KT-555-533

MORE THAN
Gold

MORE THAN
GOLD
2014

SCOTTISH
BIBLE SOCIETY
The Word for the world

Biblica™

THE GOSPEL OF LUKE
NEW INTERNATIONAL VERSION

CONTENTS

MORE THAN Gold

This book tells the real life stories of six people: Kirsty Balfour, a Scot who unexpectedly discovered a talent for swimming; Ernst van Dyk, a South African born without lower limbs who overcame the odds to win gold at the Paralympics; Dieudonné Disi, a survivor of the Rwandan genocide who was inspired to run for his country; Nick Willis, a New Zealand middle distance runner who candidly talks about the joy of winning and the sorrow of losing; and Christine Ohuruogu, a British Olympian and record holder who credits God for her success – five lives that have been influenced and affected by the sixth, the life of Jesus Christ.

Kirsty Balfour
SCOTLAND

By her own admission Kirsty Balfour (now Kettles) didn't set out to become a gold medal-winning swimmer – "It wasn't something that growing up I thought I'd ever be," she says. Part of a sporting family – her father was a triathlete – Kirsty's first taste of success was at the age of ten when she became the Scottish orienteering champion. However, when she was twelve her father enrolled her in a swimming club where a coach identified her natural ability at breaststroke, a talent Kirsty believes came from God.

"Breaststroke is about timing and co-ordination. You either have it or you don't. From an early age I had that talent, which I believe was a God-given talent."

Kirsty became a Christian when she was seven years old, asking her mother to pray with her one evening that she would be forgiven and come to know Jesus better. In the years that followed she found her faith and her swimming became increasingly intertwined. She saw the rigorous training required and the sacrifices she had to make as an opportunity to use the talent that God had given to her.

Established as one of the world's top swimmers, winning gold and silver at European, World and Commonwealth level, Kirsty approached the 2008 Beijing Olympic Games

"You have the perspective in life that God is in control."

as a medal favourite for the 200 metre breaststroke. But on the day of the crucial heats her time was slower than she hoped and she failed to make the semi-finals. Looking back, she acknowledges the pain of losing out in a race, but she is also certain that her faith in God carried her through the disappointments as well as the triumphs of her sporting career.

"You have the perspective in life that God is in control. You can only do what you can do, but you can't influence what anybody else does. So you just get in and do your best. I definitely think having faith helps to deal with the disappointment." Kirsty is convinced that nothing happens by accident, and she has always tried to see challenges as opportunities – God offering her the chance to learn something valuable.

Now a wife and mother, Kirsty describes her years of training as a 'classroom for life' where she learnt about God, herself and her relationships with others. She sums this up as "discipline, sacrifice, courage and determination" – all characteristics we read about in the life of Jesus Christ.

THE STORY OF
Jesus Christ

Jesus Christ was born a Jew in a remote outpost of the Roman Empire. He spoke predominantly to Jews and never left his homeland. Yet during this time, he befriended the untouchables of his day, broke social codes so that he could sit down with con artists, lepers and prostitutes and carried out healings so miraculous that people came out to see him in their thousands.

Thirty years after his death, Jesus' extraordinary life story was chronicled by a non-Jewish doctor we know only as Luke. Luke's account is comprehensive and factual; he simply puts what he knows out there and allows the reader to make up his or her own mind about the true identity of Jesus Christ.

THE GOSPEL
OF LUKE

INTRODUCTION

1 Many have undertaken to draw up an account of the things that have been fulfilled among us, ²just as they were handed down to us by those who from the first were eye witnesses and servants of the word. ³With this in mind, since I myself have carefully investigated everything from the beginning, I too decided to write an orderly account for you, most excellent Theophilus, ⁴so that you may know the certainty of the things you have been taught.

THE BIRTH OF JOHN THE BAPTIST FORETOLD

⁵In the time of Herod king of Judea there was a priest named Zechariah, who belonged to the priestly division of Abijah; his wife Elizabeth was also a descendant of Aaron. ⁶Both of them were righteous in the sight of God, observing all the Lord's commands and decrees blamelessly. ⁷But they were childless because Elizabeth was not able to conceive, and they were both very old.

⁸Once when Zechariah's division was on duty and he was serving as priest before God, ⁹he was chosen by lot, according to the custom of the priesthood, to go into the temple of the Lord and burn incense. ¹⁰And when the time for the burning of incense came, all the assembled worshippers were praying outside.

¹¹Then an angel of the Lord appeared to him, standing at the right side of the altar of incense. ¹²When Zechariah saw him, he was startled and was gripped with fear. ¹³But the angel said to him: 'Do not be afraid, Zechariah; your prayer has been heard. Your wife Elizabeth will bear you a son, and you are to call him John. ¹⁴He will be a joy and delight to you, and many will rejoice because of his birth, ¹⁵for he will be great in the sight of the Lord. He is never to take wine or other fermented drink, and he will be filled with the Holy Spirit even before he is born. ¹⁶He will bring back many of the people of Israel to the Lord their God. ¹⁷And he will go on before the Lord, in the spirit and power of Elijah, to turn the hearts of the parents to their children and the disobedient to the wisdom of the righteous – to make ready a people prepared for the Lord.'

¹⁸Zechariah asked the angel, 'How can I be sure of this? I am an old man and my wife is well on in years.'

¹⁹The angel said to him, 'I am Gabriel. I stand in the presence of God, and I have been sent to speak to you and to tell you this good news. ²⁰And now you will be silent and not able to speak until the day this happens, because you did not believe my words, which will come true at their appointed time.'

²¹Meanwhile, the people were waiting for Zechariah and wondering why he stayed so long in the temple. ²²When he came out,

he could not speak to them. They realised he had seen a vision in the temple, for he kept making signs to them but remained unable to speak.

²³When his time of service was completed, he returned home. ²⁴After this his wife Elizabeth became pregnant and for five months remained in seclusion. ²⁵'The Lord has done this for me,' she said. 'In these days he has shown his favour and taken away my disgrace among the people.'

THE BIRTH OF JESUS FORETOLD

²⁶In the sixth month of Elizabeth's pregnancy, God sent the angel Gabriel to Nazareth, a town in Galilee, ²⁷to a virgin pledged to be married to a man named Joseph, a descendant of David. The virgin's name was Mary. ²⁸The angel went to her and said, 'Greetings, you who are highly favoured! The Lord is with you.'

²⁹Mary was greatly troubled at his words and wondered what kind of greeting this might be. ³⁰But the angel said to her, 'Do not be afraid, Mary, you have found favour with God. ³¹You will conceive and give birth to a son, and you are to call him Jesus. ³²He will be great and will be called the Son of the Most High. The Lord God will give him the throne of his father David, ³³and he will reign over Jacob's descendants for ever; his kingdom will never end.'

³⁴'How will this be,' Mary asked the angel, 'since I am a virgin?'

³⁵The angel answered, 'The Holy Spirit will come on you, and the power of the Most High will overshadow you. So the holy one to be born will be called the Son of God. ³⁶Even Elizabeth your relative is going to have a child in her old age, and she who was said to be unable to conceive is in her sixth month. ³⁷For no word from God will ever fail.'

³⁸'I am the Lord's servant,' Mary answered. 'May your word to me be fulfilled.' Then the angel left her.

MARY VISITS ELIZABETH

³⁹At that time Mary got ready and hurried to a town in the hill country of Judea, ⁴⁰where she entered Zechariah's home and greeted Elizabeth. ⁴¹When Elizabeth heard Mary's greeting, the baby leaped in her womb, and Elizabeth was filled with the Holy Spirit. ⁴²In a loud voice she exclaimed: 'Blessed are you among women, and blessed is the child you will bear! ⁴³But why am I so favoured, that the mother of my Lord should come to me? ⁴⁴As soon as the sound of your greeting reached my ears, the baby in my womb leaped for joy. ⁴⁵Blessed is she who has believed that the Lord would fulfil his promises to her!'

MARY'S SONG

46 And Mary said:

'My soul glorifies the Lord
47 and my spirit rejoices in God my Saviour,
48 for he has been mindful
    of the humble state of his servant.
  From now on all generations will call me blessed,
49   for the Mighty One has done great things for me –
    holy is his name.
50 His mercy extends to those who fear him,
    from generation to generation.
51 He has performed mighty deeds with his arm;
    he has scattered those who are proud in their inmost thoughts.
52 He has brought down rulers from their thrones
    but has lifted up the humble.
53 He has filled the hungry with good things
    but has sent the rich away empty.
54 He has helped his servant Israel,
    remembering to be merciful
55 to Abraham and his descendants for ever,
    just as he promised our ancestors.'

56 Mary stayed with Elizabeth for about three months and then returned home.

THE BIRTH OF JOHN THE BAPTIST

57 When it was time for Elizabeth to have her baby, she gave birth to a son. 58 Her neighbours and relatives heard that the Lord had shown her great mercy, and they shared her joy.

59 On the eighth day they came to circumcise the child, and they were going to name him after his father Zechariah, 60 but his mother spoke up and said, 'No! He is to be called John.'

61 They said to her, 'There is no one among your relatives who has that name.'

62 Then they made signs to his father, to find out what he would like to name the child. 63 He asked for a writing tablet, and to everyone's astonishment he wrote, 'His name is John.' 64 Immediately his mouth was opened and his tongue set free, and he began to speak, praising God. 65 All the neighbours were filled with awe, and throughout the hill country of Judea people were talking about all these things. 66 Everyone who heard this wondered about it, asking, 'What then is this child going to be?' For the Lord's hand was with him.

ZECHARIAH'S SONG

67 His father Zechariah was filled with the Holy Spirit and prophesied:

68 'Praise be to the Lord, the God of Israel,
    because he has come to his people and redeemed them.
69 He has raised up a horn of salvation for us
    in the house of his servant David
70 (as he said through his holy prophets of long ago),
71 salvation from our enemies
    and from the hand of all who hate us –
72 to show mercy to our ancestors
    and to remember his holy covenant,
73 the oath he swore to our father Abraham:
74 to rescue us from the hand of our enemies,
    and to enable us to serve him without fear
75 in holiness and righteousness before him all our days.

76 And you, my child, will be called a prophet of the Most High;
    for you will go on before the Lord to prepare the way for him,
77 to give his people the knowledge of salvation
    through the forgiveness of their sins,
78 because of the tender mercy of our God,
    by which the rising sun will come to us from heaven
79 to shine on those living in darkness
    and in the shadow of death,
    to guide our feet into the path of peace.'

80 And the child grew and became strong in spirit; and he lived in the wilderness until he appeared publicly to Israel.

THE BIRTH OF JESUS

2 In those days Caesar Augustus issued a decree that a census should be taken of the entire Roman world. **2** (This was the first census that took place while Quirinius was governor of Syria.) **3** And everyone went to their own town to register.

4 So Joseph also went up from the town of Nazareth in Galilee to Judea, to Bethlehem the town of David, because he belonged to the house and line of David. **5** He went there to register with Mary, who was pledged to be married to him and was expecting a child. **6** While they were there, the time came for the baby to be born, **7** and she gave birth to her firstborn, a son. She wrapped him in cloths and placed him in a manger, because there was no guest room available for them.

8 And there were shepherds living out in the fields near by, keeping watch over their flocks at night. **9** An angel of the Lord appeared to them, and the glory of the Lord shone around them, and they were terrified. ¹⁰But the angel said to them, 'Do not be afraid. I bring you good news that will cause great joy for all the people. ¹¹Today in the town of David a Saviour has been born to you; he is the Messiah, the Lord. ¹²This will be a sign to you: you will find a baby wrapped in cloths and lying in a manger.'

¹³Suddenly a great company of the heavenly host appeared with the angel, praising God and saying,

¹⁴ 'Glory to God in the highest heaven,
    and on earth peace to those on whom his favour rests.'

¹⁵When the angels had left them and gone into heaven, the shepherds said to one another, 'Let's go to Bethlehem and see this thing that has happened, which the Lord has told us about.'

¹⁶So they hurried off and found Mary and Joseph, and the baby, who was lying in the manger. ¹⁷When they had seen him, they spread the word concerning what had been told them about this child, ¹⁸and all who heard it were amazed at what the shepherds said to them. ¹⁹But Mary treasured up all these things and pondered them in her heart. ²⁰The shepherds returned, glorifying and praising God for all the things they had heard and seen, which were just as they had been told.

²¹On the eighth day, when it was time to circumcise the child, he was named Jesus, the name the angel had given him before he was conceived.

JESUS PRESENTED IN THE TEMPLE

²²When the time came for the purification rites required by the Law of Moses, Joseph and Mary took him to Jerusalem to present him to the Lord ²³(as it is written in the Law of the Lord, 'Every firstborn male is to be consecrated to the Lord'), ²⁴and to offer a sacrifice in keeping with what is said in the Law of the Lord: 'a pair of doves or two young pigeons'.

²⁵Now there was a man in Jerusalem called Simeon, who was righteous and devout. He was waiting for the consolation of Israel, and the Holy Spirit was on him. ²⁶It had been revealed to him by the Holy Spirit that he would not die before he had seen the Lord's Messiah. ²⁷Moved by the Spirit, he went into the temple courts. When the parents brought in the child Jesus to do for him what the custom of the Law required, ²⁸Simeon took him in his arms and praised God, saying:

²⁹ 'Sovereign Lord, as you have promised,
    you may now dismiss your servant in peace.
³⁰ For my eyes have seen your salvation,

31 which you have prepared in the sight of all nations:
32 a light for revelation to the Gentiles,
   and the glory of your people Israel.'

33 The child's father and mother marvelled at what was said about him. 34 Then Simeon blessed them and said to Mary, his mother: 'This child is destined to cause the falling and rising of many in Israel, and to be a sign that will be spoken against, 35 so that the thoughts of many hearts will be revealed. And a sword will pierce your own soul too.'

36 There was also a prophet, Anna, the daughter of Penuel, of the tribe of Asher. She was very old; she had lived with her husband seven years after her marriage, 37 and then was a widow until she was eighty-four. She never left the temple but worshipped night and day, fasting and praying. 38 Coming up to them at that very moment, she gave thanks to God and spoke about the child to all who were looking forward to the redemption of Jerusalem.

39 When Joseph and Mary had done everything required by the Law of the Lord, they returned to Galilee to their own town of Nazareth. 40 And the child grew and became strong; he was filled with wisdom, and the grace of God was on him.

THE BOY JESUS AT THE TEMPLE

41 Every year Jesus' parents went to Jerusalem for the Festival of the Passover. 42 When he was twelve years old, they went up to the festival, according to the custom. 43 After the festival was over, while his parents were returning home, the boy Jesus stayed behind in Jerusalem, but they were unaware of it. 44 Thinking he was in their company, they travelled on for a day. Then they began looking for him among their relatives and friends. 45 When they did not find him, they went back to Jerusalem to look for him. 46 After three days they found him in the temple courts, sitting among the teachers, listening to them and asking them questions. 47 Everyone who heard him was amazed at his understanding and his answers. 48 When his parents saw him, they were astonished. His mother said to him, 'Son, why have you treated us like this? Your father and I have been anxiously searching for you.'

49 'Why were you searching for me?' he asked. 'Didn't you know I had to be in my Father's house?' 50 But they did not understand what he was saying to them.

51 Then he went down to Nazareth with them and was obedient to them. But his mother treasured all these things in her heart. 52 And Jesus grew in wisdom and stature, and in favour with God and man.

JOHN THE BAPTIST PREPARES THE WAY

3 In the fifteenth year of the reign of Tiberius Caesar – when Pontius Pilate was governor of Judea, Herod tetrarch of Galilee, his brother Philip tetrarch of Iturea and Traconitis, and Lysanias tetrarch of Abilene – 2during the high-priesthood of Annas and Caiaphas, the word of God came to John son of Zechariah in the wilderness. 3He went into all the country around the Jordan, preaching a baptism of repentance for the forgiveness of sins. 4As it is written in the book of the words of Isaiah the prophet:

'A voice of one calling in the wilderness,
"Prepare the way for the Lord,
    make straight paths for him.
5 Every valley shall be filled in,
        every mountain and hill made low.
The crooked roads shall become straight,
        the rough ways smooth.
6   And all people will see God's salvation." '

7John said to the crowds coming out to be baptised by him, 'You brood of vipers! Who warned you to flee from the coming wrath? 8Produce fruit in keeping with repentance. And do not begin to say to yourselves, "We have Abraham as our father." For I tell you that out of these stones God can raise up children for Abraham. 9The axe has been laid to the root of the trees, and every tree that does not produce good fruit will be cut down and thrown into the fire.'

10'What should we do then?' the crowd asked.

11John answered, 'Anyone who has two shirts should share with the one who has none, and anyone who has food should do the same.'

12Even tax collectors came to be baptised. 'Teacher,' they asked, 'what should we do?'

13'Don't collect any more than you are required to,' he told them. 14Then some soldiers asked him, 'And what should we do?'

He replied, 'Don't extort money and don't accuse people falsely – be content with your pay.'

15The people were waiting expectantly and were all wondering in their hearts if John might possibly be the Messiah. 16John answered them all, 'I baptise you with water. But one who is more powerful than I will come, the straps of whose sandals I am not worthy to untie. He will baptise you with the Holy Spirit and fire. 17His winnowing fork is in his hand to clear his threshing-floor and to gather the wheat into his barn, but he will burn up the chaff with unquenchable fire.' 18And with many other words John exhorted the people and proclaimed the good news to them.

¹⁹But when John rebuked Herod the tetrarch because of his marriage to Herodias, his brother's wife, and all the other evil things he had done, ²⁰Herod added this to them all: he locked John up in prison.

THE BAPTISM AND GENEALOGY OF JESUS

²¹When all the people were being baptised, Jesus was baptised too. And as he was praying, heaven was opened ²²and the Holy Spirit descended on him in bodily form like a dove. And a voice came from heaven: 'You are my Son, whom I love; with you I am well pleased.'

²³Now Jesus himself was about thirty years old when he began his ministry. He was the son, so it was thought, of Joseph,

the son of Heli, ²⁴the son of Matthat,
the son of Levi, the son of Melki,
the son of Jannai, the son of Joseph,
²⁵the son of Mattathias, the son of Amos,
the son of Nahum, the son of Esli,
the son of Naggai, ²⁶the son of Maath,
the son of Mattathias, the son of Semein,
the son of Josek, the son of Joda,
²⁷the son of Joanan, the son of Rhesa,
the son of Zerubbabel, the son of Shealtiel,
the son of Neri, ²⁸the son of Melki,
the son of Addi, the son of Cosam,
the son of Elmadam, the son of Er,
²⁹the son of Joshua, the son of Eliezer,
the son of Jorim, the son of Matthat,
the son of Levi, ³⁰the son of Simeon,
the son of Judah, the son of Joseph,
the son of Jonam, the son of Eliakim,
³¹the son of Melea, the son of Menna,
the son of Mattatha, the son of Nathan,
the son of David, ³²the son of Jesse,
the son of Obed, the son of Boaz,
the son of Salmon, the son of Nahshon,
³³the son of Amminadab, the son of Ram,
the son of Hezron, the son of Perez,
the son of Judah, ³⁴the son of Jacob,
the son of Isaac, the son of Abraham,
the son of Terah, the son of Nahor,
³⁵the son of Serug, the son of Reu,
the son of Peleg, the son of Eber,
the son of Shelah, ³⁶the son of Cainan,

the son of Arphaxad, the son of Shem,
the son of Noah, the son of Lamech,
37 the son of Methuselah, the son of Enoch,
the son of Jared, the son of Mahalalel,
the son of Kenan, 38 the son of Enosh,
the son of Seth, the son of Adam,
the son of God.

JESUS IS TESTED IN THE WILDERNESS

4 Jesus, full of the Holy Spirit, left the Jordan and was led by the Spirit into the wilderness, 2 where for forty days he was tempted by the devil. He ate nothing during those days, and at the end of them he was hungry.

3 The devil said to him, 'If you are the Son of God, tell this stone to become bread.'

4 Jesus answered, 'It is written: "Man shall not live on bread alone."'

5 The devil led him up to a high place and showed him in an instant all the kingdoms of the world. 6 And he said to him, 'I will give you all their authority and splendour; it has been given to me, and I can give it to anyone I want to. 7 If you worship me, it will all be yours.'

8 Jesus answered, 'It is written: "Worship the Lord your God and serve him only."'

9 The devil led him to Jerusalem and had him stand on the highest point of the temple. 'If you are the Son of God,' he said, 'throw yourself down from here. 10 For it is written:

' "He will command his angels concerning you
     to guard you carefully;
11 they will lift you up in their hands,
     so that you will not strike your foot against a stone."'

12 Jesus answered, 'It is said: "Do not put the Lord your God to the test."'

13 When the devil had finished all this tempting, he left him until an opportune time.

JESUS REJECTED AT NAZARETH

14 Jesus returned to Galilee in the power of the Spirit, and news about him spread through the whole countryside. 15 He was teaching in their synagogues, and everyone praised him.

16 He went to Nazareth, where he had been brought up, and on the Sabbath day he went into the synagogue, as was his custom. He stood up to read, 17 and the scroll of the prophet Isaiah was handed to him. Unrolling it, he found the place where it is written:

18 'The Spirit of the Lord is on me,
    because he has anointed me
      to proclaim good news to the poor.
  He has sent me to proclaim freedom for the prisoners
      and recovery of sight for the blind,
        to set the oppressed free,
19 to proclaim the year of the Lord's favour.'

20 Then he rolled up the scroll, gave it back to the attendant and sat down. The eyes of everyone in the synagogue were fastened on him. 21 He began by saying to them, 'Today this scripture is fulfilled in your hearing.'

22 All spoke well of him and were amazed at the gracious words that came from his lips. 'Isn't this Joseph's son?' they asked.

23 Jesus said to them, 'Surely you will quote this proverb to me: "Physician, heal yourself!" And you will tell me, "Do here in your home town what we have heard that you did in Capernaum."'

24 'Truly I tell you,' he continued, 'no prophet is accepted in his home town. 25 I assure you that there were many widows in Israel in Elijah's time, when the sky was shut for three and a half years and there was a severe famine throughout the land. 26 Yet Elijah was not sent to any of them, but to a widow in Zarephath in the region of Sidon. 27 And there were many in Israel with leprosy in the time of Elisha the prophet, yet not one of them was cleansed – only Naaman the Syrian.'

28 All the people in the synagogue were furious when they heard this. 29 They got up, drove him out of the town, and took him to the brow of the hill on which the town was built, in order to throw him off the cliff. 30 But he walked right through the crowd and went on his way.

JESUS DRIVES OUT AN IMPURE SPIRIT

31 Then he went down to Capernaum, a town in Galilee, and on the Sabbath he taught the people. 32 They were amazed at his teaching, because his words had authority.

33 In the synagogue there was a man possessed by a demon, an impure spirit. He cried out at the top of his voice, 34 'Go away! What do you want with us, Jesus of Nazareth? Have you come to destroy us? I know who you are – the Holy One of God!'

35 'Be quiet!' Jesus said sternly. 'Come out of him!' Then the demon threw the man down before them all and came out without injuring him.

36 All the people were amazed and said to each other, 'What words these are! With authority and power he gives orders to impure spirits and they come out!' 37 And the news about him spread throughout the surrounding area.

JESUS HEALS MANY

38 Jesus left the synagogue and went to the home of Simon. Now Simon's mother-in-law was suffering from a high fever, and they asked Jesus to help her. 39 So he bent over her and rebuked the fever, and it left her. She got up at once and began to wait on them.

40 At sunset, the people brought to Jesus all who had various kinds of illness, and laying his hands on each one, he healed them. 41 Moreover, demons came out of many people, shouting, 'You are the Son of God!' But he rebuked them and would not allow them to speak, because they knew he was the Messiah.

42 At daybreak, Jesus went out to a solitary place. The people were looking for him and when they came to where he was, they tried to keep him from leaving them. 43 But he said, 'I must proclaim the good news of the kingdom of God to the other towns also, because that is why I was sent.' 44 And he kept on preaching in the synagogues of Judea.

JESUS CALLS HIS FIRST DISCIPLES

5 One day as Jesus was standing by the Lake of Gennesaret, the people were crowding round him and listening to the word of God. 2 He saw at the water's edge two boats, left there by the fishermen, who were washing their nets. 3 He got into one of the boats, the one belonging to Simon, and asked him to put out a little from the shore. Then he sat down and taught the people from the boat.

4 When he had finished speaking, he said to Simon, 'Put out into deep water, and let down the nets for a catch.'

5 Simon answered, 'Master, we've worked hard all night and haven't caught anything. But because you say so, I will let down the nets.'

6 When they had done so, they caught such a large number of fish that their nets began to break. 7 So they signalled to their partners in the other boat to come and help them, and they came and filled both boats so full that they began to sink.

8 When Simon Peter saw this, he fell at Jesus' knees and said, 'Go away from me, Lord; I am a sinful man!' 9 For he and all his companions were astonished at the catch of fish they had taken, 10 and so were James and John, the sons of Zebedee, Simon's partners.

Then Jesus said to Simon, 'Don't be afraid; from now on you will fish for people.' 11 So they pulled their boats up on shore, left everything and followed him.

JESUS HEALS A MAN WITH LEPROSY

12 While Jesus was in one of the towns, a man came along who was covered with leprosy. When he saw Jesus, he fell with his face

to the ground and begged him, 'Lord, if you are willing, you can make me clean.'

13 Jesus reached out his hand and touched the man. 'I am willing,' he said. 'Be clean!' And immediately the leprosy left him.

14 Then Jesus ordered him, 'Don't tell anyone, but go, show yourself to the priest and offer the sacrifices that Moses commanded for your cleansing, as a testimony to them.'

15 Yet the news about him spread all the more, so that crowds of people came to hear him and to be healed of their illnesses. 16 But Jesus often withdrew to lonely places and prayed.

JESUS FORGIVES AND HEALS A PARALYSED MAN

17 One day Jesus was teaching, and Pharisees and teachers of the law were sitting there. They had come from every village of Galilee and from Judea and Jerusalem. And the power of the Lord was with Jesus to heal those who were ill. 18 Some men came carrying a paralysed man on a mat and tried to take him into the house to lay him before Jesus. 19 When they could not find a way to do this because of the crowd, they went up on the roof and lowered him on his mat through the tiles into the middle of the crowd, right in front of Jesus.

20 When Jesus saw their faith, he said, 'Friend, your sins are forgiven.'

21 The Pharisees and the teachers of the law began thinking to themselves, 'Who is this fellow who speaks blasphemy? Who can forgive sins but God alone?'

22 Jesus knew what they were thinking and asked, 'Why are you thinking these things in your hearts? 23 Which is easier: to say, "Your sins are forgiven," or to say, "Get up and walk"? 24 But I want you to know that the Son of Man has authority on earth to forgive sins.' So he said to the paralysed man, 'I tell you, get up, take your mat and go home.' 25 Immediately he stood up in front of them, took what he had been lying on and went home praising God. 26 Everyone was amazed and gave praise to God. They were filled with awe and said, 'We have seen remarkable things today.'

JESUS CALLS LEVI AND EATS WITH SINNERS

27 After this, Jesus went out and saw a tax collector by the name of Levi sitting at his tax booth. 'Follow me,' Jesus said to him, 28 and Levi got up, left everything and followed him.

29 Then Levi held a great banquet for Jesus at his house, and a large crowd of tax collectors and others were eating with them. 30 But the Pharisees and the teachers of the law who belonged to their sect complained to his disciples, 'Why do you eat and drink with tax collectors and sinners?'

31 Jesus answered them, 'It is not the healthy who need a doctor, but those who are ill. **32** I have not come to call the righteous, but sinners to repentance.'

JESUS QUESTIONED ABOUT FASTING

33 They said to him, 'John's disciples often fast and pray, and so do the disciples of the Pharisees, but yours go on eating and drinking.'

34 Jesus answered, 'Can you make the friends of the bridegroom fast while he is with them? **35** But the time will come when the bridegroom will be taken from them; in those days they will fast.'

36 He told them this parable: 'No one tears a piece out of a new garment to patch an old one. Otherwise, they will have torn the new garment, and the patch from the new will not match the old. **37** And no one pours new wine into old wineskins. Otherwise, the new wine will burst the skins; the wine will run out and the wineskins will be ruined. **38** No, new wine must be poured into new wineskins. **39** And no one after drinking old wine wants the new, for they say, "The old is better."'

JESUS IS LORD OF THE SABBATH

6 One Sabbath Jesus was going through the cornfields, and his disciples began to pick some ears of corn, rub them in their hands and eat the grain. **2** Some of the Pharisees asked, 'Why are you doing what is unlawful on the Sabbath?'

3 Jesus answered them, 'Have you never read what David did when he and his companions were hungry? **4** He entered the house of God, and taking the consecrated bread, he ate what is lawful only for priests to eat. And he also gave some to his companions.' **5** Then Jesus said to them, 'The Son of Man is Lord of the Sabbath.'

6 On another Sabbath he went into the synagogue and was teaching, and a man was there whose right hand was shrivelled. **7** The Pharisees and the teachers of the law were looking for a reason to accuse Jesus, so they watched him closely to see if he would heal on the Sabbath. **8** But Jesus knew what they were thinking and said to the man with the shrivelled hand, 'Get up and stand in front of everyone.' So he got up and stood there.

9 Then Jesus said to them, 'I ask you, which is lawful on the Sabbath: to do good or to do evil, to save life or to destroy it?'

10 He looked round at them all, and then said to the man, 'Stretch out your hand.' He did so, and his hand was completely restored. **11** But the Pharisees and the teachers of the law were furious and began to discuss with one another what they might do to Jesus.

THE TWELVE APOSTLES

12 One of those days Jesus went out to a mountainside to pray, and spent the night praying to God. **13** When morning came, he called his disciples to him and chose twelve of them, whom he also designated apostles: **14** Simon (whom he named Peter), his brother Andrew, James, John, Philip, Bartholomew, **15** Matthew, Thomas, James son of Alphaeus, Simon who was called the Zealot, **16** Judas son of James, and Judas Iscariot, who became a traitor.

BLESSINGS AND WOES

17 He went down with them and stood on a level place. A large crowd of his disciples was there and a great number of people from all over Judea, from Jerusalem, and from the coastal region around Tyre and Sidon, **18** who had come to hear him and to be healed of their diseases. Those troubled by impure spirits were cured, **19** and the people all tried to touch him, because power was coming from him and healing them all.

20 Looking at his disciples, he said:

'Blessed are you who are poor,
　for yours is the kingdom of God.
21 Blessed are you who hunger now,
　for you will be satisfied.
Blessed are you who weep now,
　for you will laugh.
22 Blessed are you when people hate you,
　when they exclude you and insult you
and reject your name as evil,
　because of the Son of Man.

23 'Rejoice in that day and leap for joy, because great is your reward in heaven. For that is how their ancestors treated the prophets.

24 'But woe to you who are rich,
　for you have already received your comfort.
25 Woe to you who are well fed now,
　for you will go hungry.
Woe to you who laugh now,
　for you will mourn and weep.
26 Woe to you when everyone speaks well of you,
　for that is how their ancestors treated the false prophets.

LOVE FOR ENEMIES

27 'But to you who are listening I say: love your enemies, do good to those who hate you, **28** bless those who curse you, pray for those who ill-treat you. 29 If someone slaps you on one cheek, turn to them the other also. If someone takes your coat, do not withhold your shirt from them. 30 Give to everyone who asks you, and if anyone takes what belongs to you, do not demand it back. 31 Do to others as you would have them do to you.

32 'If you love those who love you, what credit is that to you? Even sinners love those who love them. 33 And if you do good to those who are good to you, what credit is that to you? Even sinners do that. 34 And if you lend to those from whom you expect repayment, what credit is that to you? Even sinners lend to sinners, expecting to be repaid in full. 35 But love your enemies, do good to them, and lend to them without expecting to get anything back. Then your reward will be great, and you will be children of the Most High, because he is kind to the ungrateful and wicked. 36 Be merciful, just as your Father is merciful.

JUDGING OTHERS

37 'Do not judge, and you will not be judged. Do not condemn, and you will not be condemned. Forgive, and you will be forgiven. 38 Give, and it will be given to you. A good measure, pressed down, shaken together and running over, will be poured into your lap. For with the measure you use, it will be measured to you.'

39 He also told them this parable: 'Can the blind lead the blind? Will they not both fall into a pit? 40 The student is not above the teacher, but everyone who is fully trained will be like their teacher.

41 'Why do you look at the speck of sawdust in your brother's eye and pay no attention to the plank in your own eye? 42 How can you say to your brother, "Brother, let me take the speck out of your eye," when you yourself fail to see the plank in your own eye? You hypocrite, first take the plank out of your eye, and then you will see clearly to remove the speck from your brother's eye.

A TREE AND ITS FRUIT

43 'No good tree bears bad fruit, nor does a bad tree bear good fruit. 44 Each tree is recognised by its own fruit. People do not pick figs from thorn-bushes, or grapes from briers. 45 A good man brings good things out of the good stored up in his heart, and an evil man brings evil things out of the evil stored up in his heart. For the mouth speaks what the heart is full of.

THE WISE AND FOOLISH BUILDERS

46 'Why do you call me, "Lord, Lord," and do not do what I say? 47 As for everyone who comes to me and hears my words and puts them into practice, I will show you what they are like. 48 They are like a man building a house, who dug down deep and laid the

foundation on rock. When the flood came, the torrent struck that house but could not shake it, because it was well built. **49**But the one who hears my words and does not put them into practice is like a man who built a house on the ground without a foundation. The moment the torrent struck that house, it collapsed and its destruction was complete.'

THE FAITH OF THE CENTURION

7 When Jesus had finished saying all this to the people who were listening, he entered Capernaum. **2**There a centurion's servant, whom his master valued highly, was ill and about to die. **3**The centurion heard of Jesus and sent some elders of the Jews to him, asking him to come and heal his servant. **4**When they came to Jesus, they pleaded earnestly with him, 'This man deserves to have you do this, **5**because he loves our nation and has built our synagogue.' **6**So Jesus went with them.

He was not far from the house when the centurion sent friends to say to him: 'Lord, don't trouble yourself, for I do not deserve to have you come under my roof. **7**That is why I did not even consider myself worthy to come to you. But say the word, and my servant will be healed. **8**For I myself am a man under authority, with soldiers under me. I tell this one, "Go", and he goes; and that one, "Come", and he comes. I say to my servant, "Do this", and he does it.'

9When Jesus heard this, he was amazed at him, and turning to the crowd following him, he said, 'I tell you, I have not found such great faith even in Israel.' **10**Then the men who had been sent returned to the house and found the servant well.

JESUS RAISES A WIDOW'S SON

11Soon afterwards, Jesus went to a town called Nain, and his disciples and a large crowd went along with him. **12**As he approached the town gate, a dead person was being carried out – the only son of his mother, and she was a widow. And a large crowd from the town was with her. **13**When the Lord saw her, his heart went out to her and he said, 'Don't cry.'

14Then he went up and touched the bier they were carrying him on, and the bearers stood still. He said, 'Young man, I say to you, get up!' **15**The dead man sat up and began to talk, and Jesus gave him back to his mother.

16They were all filled with awe and praised God. 'A great prophet has appeared among us,' they said. 'God has come to help his people.' **17**This news about Jesus spread throughout Judea and the surrounding country.

JESUS AND JOHN THE BAPTIST

18 John's disciples told him about all these things. Calling two of them, **19** he sent them to the Lord to ask, 'Are you the one who is to come, or should we expect someone else?'

20 When the men came to Jesus, they said, 'John the Baptist sent us to you to ask, "Are you the one who is to come, or should we expect someone else?"'

21 At that very time Jesus cured many who had diseases, illnesses and evil spirits, and gave sight to many who were blind. **22** So he replied to the messengers, 'Go back and report to John what you have seen and heard: the blind receive sight, the lame walk, those who have leprosy are cleansed, the deaf hear, the dead are raised, and the good news is proclaimed to the poor. **23** Blessed is anyone who does not stumble on account of me.'

24 After John's messengers left, Jesus began to speak to the crowd about John: 'What did you go out into the wilderness to see? A reed swayed by the wind? **25** If not, what did you go out to see? A man dressed in fine clothes? No, those who wear expensive clothes and indulge in luxury are in palaces. **26** But what did you go out to see? A prophet? Yes, I tell you, and more than a prophet. **27** This is the one about whom it is written:

' "I will send my messenger ahead of you,
    who will prepare your way before you."

28 I tell you, among those born of women there is no one greater than John; yet the one who is least in the kingdom of God is greater than he.'

29 (All the people, even the tax collectors, when they heard Jesus' words, acknowledged that God's way was right, because they had been baptised by John. **30** But the Pharisees and the experts in the law rejected God's purpose for themselves, because they had not been baptised by John.)

31 Jesus went on to say, 'To what, then, can I compare the people of this generation? What are they like? **32** They are like children sitting in the market-place and calling out to each other:

' "We played the pipe for you,
    and you did not dance;
we sang a dirge,
    and you did not cry."

33 For John the Baptist came neither eating bread nor drinking wine, and you say, "He has a demon." **34** The Son of Man came eating and drinking, and you say, "Here is a glutton and a drunkard, a friend of tax collectors and sinners." **35** But wisdom is proved right by all her children.'

JESUS ANOINTED BY A SINFUL WOMAN

36When one of the Pharisees invited Jesus to have dinner with him, he went to the Pharisee's house and reclined at the table. 37A woman in that town who lived a sinful life learned that Jesus was eating at the Pharisee's house, so she came there with an alabaster jar of perfume. 38As she stood behind him at his feet weeping, she began to wet his feet with her tears. Then she wiped them with her hair, kissed them and poured perfume on them.

39When the Pharisee who had invited him saw this, he said to himself, 'If this man were a prophet, he would know who is touching him and what kind of woman she is – that she is a sinner.'

40Jesus answered him, 'Simon, I have something to tell you.'

'Tell me, teacher,' he said.

41'Two people owed money to a certain money-lender. One owed him five hundred denarii, and the other fifty. 42Neither of them had the money to pay him back, so he forgave the debts of both. Now which of them will love him more?'

43Simon replied, 'I suppose the one who had the bigger debt forgiven.'

'You have judged correctly,' Jesus said.

44Then he turned towards the woman and said to Simon, 'Do you see this woman? I came into your house. You did not give me any water for my feet, but she wet my feet with her tears and wiped them with her hair. 45You did not give me a kiss, but this woman, from the time I entered, has not stopped kissing my feet. 46You did not put oil on my head, but she has poured perfume on my feet. 47Therefore, I tell you, her many sins have been forgiven – as her great love has shown. But whoever has been forgiven little loves little.'

48Then Jesus said to her, 'Your sins are forgiven.'

49The other guests began to say among themselves, 'Who is this who even forgives sins?'

50Jesus said to the woman, 'Your faith has saved you; go in peace.'

THE PARABLE OF THE SOWER

8 After this, Jesus travelled about from one town and village to another, proclaiming the good news of the kingdom of God. The Twelve were with him, 2and also some women who had been cured of evil spirits and diseases: Mary (called Magdalene) from whom seven demons had come out; 3Joanna the wife of Chuza, the manager of Herod's household; Susanna; and many others. These women were helping to support them out of their own means.

⁴While a large crowd was gathering and people were coming to Jesus from town after town, he told this parable: ⁵'A farmer went out to sow his seed. As he was scattering the seed, some fell along the path; it was trampled on, and the birds ate it up. ⁶Some fell on rocky ground, and when it came up, the plants withered because they had no moisture. ⁷Other seed fell among thorns, which grew up with it and choked the plants. ⁸Still other seed fell on good soil. It came up and yielded a crop, a hundred times more than was sown.'

When he said this, he called out, 'Whoever has ears to hear, let them hear.'

⁹His disciples asked him what this parable meant. ¹⁰He said, 'The knowledge of the secrets of the kingdom of God has been given to you, but to others I speak in parables, so that,

' "though seeing, they may not see;
   though hearing, they may not understand."'

¹¹'This is the meaning of the parable: the seed is the word of God. ¹²Those along the path are the ones who hear, and then the devil comes and takes away the word from their hearts, so that they may not believe and be saved. ¹³Those on the rocky ground are the ones who receive the word with joy when they hear it, but they have no root. They believe for a while, but in the time of testing they fall away. ¹⁴The seed that fell among thorns stands for those who hear, but as they go on their way they are choked by life's worries, riches and pleasures, and they do not mature. ¹⁵But the seed on good soil stands for those with a noble and good heart, who hear the word, retain it, and by persevering produce a crop.

A LAMP ON A STAND

¹⁶'No one lights a lamp and hides it in a clay jar or puts it under a bed. Instead, they put it on a stand, so that those who come in can see the light. ¹⁷For there is nothing hidden that will not be disclosed, and nothing concealed that will not be known or brought out into the open. ¹⁸Therefore consider carefully how you listen. Whoever has will be given more; whoever does not have, even what they think they have will be taken from them.'

JESUS' MOTHER AND BROTHERS

¹⁹Now Jesus' mother and brothers came to see him, but they were not able to get near him because of the crowd. ²⁰Someone told him, 'Your mother and brothers are standing outside, wanting to see you.'

²¹He replied, 'My mother and brothers are those who hear God's word and put it into practice.'

JESUS CALMS THE STORM

22 One day Jesus said to his disciples, 'Let us go over to the other side of the lake.' So they got into a boat and set out. 23 As they sailed, he fell asleep. A squall came down on the lake, so that the boat was being swamped, and they were in great danger.

24 The disciples went and woke him, saying, 'Master, Master, we're going to drown!'

He got up and rebuked the wind and the raging waters; the storm subsided, and all was calm. 25 'Where is your faith?' he asked his disciples.

In fear and amazement they asked one another, 'Who is this? He commands even the winds and the water, and they obey him.'

JESUS RESTORES A DEMON-POSSESSED MAN

26 They sailed to the region of the Gerasenes, which is across the lake from Galilee. 27 When Jesus stepped ashore, he was met by a demon-possessed man from the town. For a long time this man had not worn clothes or lived in a house, but had lived in the tombs. 28 When he saw Jesus, he cried out and fell at his feet, shouting at the top of his voice, 'What do you want with me, Jesus, Son of the Most High God? I beg you, don't torture me!' 29 For Jesus had commanded the impure spirit to come out of the man. Many times it had seized him, and though he was chained hand and foot and kept under guard, he had broken his chains and had been driven by the demon into solitary places.

30 Jesus asked him, 'What is your name?'

'Legion,' he replied, because many demons had gone into him. 31 And they begged Jesus repeatedly not to order them to go into the Abyss.

32 A large herd of pigs was feeding there on the hillside. The demons begged Jesus to let them go into the pigs, and he gave them permission. 33 When the demons came out of the man, they went into the pigs, and the herd rushed down the steep bank into the lake and was drowned.

34 When those tending the pigs saw what had happened, they ran off and reported this in the town and countryside, 35 and the people went out to see what had happened. When they came to Jesus, they found the man from whom the demons had gone out, sitting at Jesus' feet, dressed and in his right mind; and they were afraid. 36 Those who had seen it told the people how the demon-possessed man had been cured. 37 Then all the people of the region of the Gerasenes asked Jesus to leave them, because they were overcome with fear. So he got into the boat and left.

38 The man from whom the demons had gone out begged to go with him, but Jesus sent him away, saying, 39 'Return home and tell

how much God has done for you.' So the man went away and told all over the town how much Jesus had done for him.

JESUS RAISES A DEAD GIRL AND HEALS A SICK WOMAN

40 Now when Jesus returned, a crowd welcomed him, for they were all expecting him. 41 Then a man named Jairus, a synagogue leader, came and fell at Jesus' feet, pleading with him to come to his house 42 because his only daughter, a girl of about twelve, was dying.

As Jesus was on his way, the crowds almost crushed him. 43 And a woman was there who had been subject to bleeding for twelve years, but no one could heal her. 44 She came up behind him and touched the edge of his cloak, and immediately her bleeding stopped.

45 'Who touched me?' Jesus asked.

When they all denied it, Peter said, 'Master, the people are crowding and pressing against you.'

46 But Jesus said, 'Someone touched me; I know that power has gone out from me.'

47 Then the woman, seeing that she could not go unnoticed, came trembling and fell at his feet. In the presence of all the people, she told why she had touched him and how she had been instantly healed. 48 Then he said to her, 'Daughter, your faith has healed you. Go in peace.'

49 While Jesus was still speaking, someone came from the house of Jairus, the synagogue leader. 'Your daughter is dead,' he said. 'Don't bother the teacher anymore.'

50 Hearing this, Jesus said to Jairus, 'Don't be afraid; just believe, and she will be healed.'

51 When he arrived at the house of Jairus, he did not let anyone go in with him except Peter, John and James, and the child's father and mother. 52 Meanwhile, all the people were wailing and mourning for her. 'Stop wailing,' Jesus said. 'She is not dead but asleep.'

53 They laughed at him, knowing that she was dead. 54 But he took her by the hand and said, 'My child, get up!' 55 Her spirit returned, and at once she stood up. Then Jesus told them to give her something to eat. 56 Her parents were astonished, but he ordered them not to tell anyone what had happened.

JESUS SENDS OUT THE TWELVE

9 When Jesus had called the Twelve together, he gave them power and authority to drive out all demons and to cure diseases, 2 and he sent them out to proclaim the kingdom of God and to heal those who were ill. 3 He told them: 'Take nothing for

the journey – no staff, no bag, no bread, no money, no extra shirt. 4Whatever house you enter, stay there until you leave that town. 5If people do not welcome you, leave their town and shake the dust off your feet as a testimony against them.' 6So they set out and went from village to village, proclaiming the good news and healing people everywhere.

7Now Herod the tetrarch heard about all that was going on. And he was perplexed because some were saying that John had been raised from the dead, 8others that Elijah had appeared, and still others that one of the prophets of long ago had come back to life. 9But Herod said, 'I beheaded John. Who, then, is this I hear such things about?' And he tried to see him.

JESUS FEEDS THE FIVE THOUSAND

10When the apostles returned, they reported to Jesus what they had done. Then he took them with him and they withdrew by themselves to a town called Bethsaida, 11but the crowds learned about it and followed him. He welcomed them and spoke to them about the kingdom of God, and healed those who needed healing.

12Late in the afternoon the Twelve came to him and said, 'Send the crowd away so they can go to the surrounding villages and countryside and find food and lodging, because we are in a remote place here.'

13He replied, 'You give them something to eat.'

They answered, 'We have only five loaves of bread and two fish – unless we go and buy food for all this crowd.' 14(About five thousand men were there.)

But he said to his disciples, 'Make them sit down in groups of about fifty each.' 15The disciples did so, and everyone sat down. 16Taking the five loaves and the two fish and looking up to heaven, he gave thanks and broke them. Then he gave them to the disciples to distribute to the people. 17They all ate and were satisfied, and the disciples picked up twelve basketfuls of broken pieces that were left over.

PETER DECLARES THAT JESUS IS THE MESSIAH

18Once when Jesus was praying in private and his disciples were with him, he asked them, 'Who do the crowds say I am?'

19They replied, 'Some say John the Baptist; others say Elijah; and still others, that one of the prophets of long ago has come back to life.'

20'But what about you?' he asked. 'Who do you say I am?'

Peter answered, 'God's Messiah.'

JESUS PREDICTS HIS DEATH

²¹ Jesus strictly warned them not to tell this to anyone. ²² And he said, 'The Son of Man must suffer many things and be rejected by the elders, the chief priests and the teachers of the law, and he must be killed and on the third day be raised to life.'

²³ Then he said to them all: 'Whoever wants to be my disciple must deny themselves and take up their cross daily and follow me. ²⁴ For whoever wants to save their life will lose it, but whoever loses their life for me will save it. ²⁵ What good is it for someone to gain the whole world, and yet lose or forfeit their very self? ²⁶ Whoever is ashamed of me and my words, the Son of Man will be ashamed of them when he comes in his glory and in the glory of the Father and of the holy angels.

²⁷ 'Truly I tell you, some who are standing here will not taste death before they see the kingdom of God.'

THE TRANSFIGURATION

²⁸ About eight days after Jesus said this, he took Peter, John and James with him and went up onto a mountain to pray. ²⁹ As he was praying, the appearance of his face changed, and his clothes became as bright as a flash of lightning. ³⁰ Two men, Moses and Elijah, appeared in glorious splendour, talking with Jesus. ³¹ They spoke about his departure, which he was about to bring to fulfilment at Jerusalem. ³² Peter and his companions were very sleepy, but when they became fully awake, they saw his glory and the two men standing with him. ³³ As the men were leaving Jesus, Peter said to him, 'Master, it is good for us to be here. Let us put up three shelters – one for you, one for Moses and one for Elijah.' (He did not know what he was saying.)

³⁴ While he was speaking, a cloud appeared and covered them, and they were afraid as they entered the cloud. ³⁵ A voice came from the cloud, saying, 'This is my Son, whom I have chosen; listen to him.' ³⁶ When the voice had spoken, they found that Jesus was alone. The disciples kept this to themselves and did not tell anyone at that time what they had seen.

JESUS HEALS A DEMON-POSSESSED BOY

³⁷ The next day, when they came down from the mountain, a large crowd met him. ³⁸ A man in the crowd called out, 'Teacher, I beg you to look at my son, for he is my only child. ³⁹ A spirit seizes him and he suddenly screams; it throws him into convulsions so that he foams at the mouth. It scarcely ever leaves him and is destroying him. ⁴⁰ I begged your disciples to drive it out, but they could not.'

⁴¹ 'You unbelieving and perverse generation,' Jesus replied, 'how long shall I stay with you and put up with you? Bring your son here.'

⁴²Even while the boy was coming, the demon threw him to the ground in a convulsion. But Jesus rebuked the impure spirit, healed the boy and gave him back to his father. ⁴³And they were all amazed at the greatness of God.

JESUS PREDICTS HIS DEATH A SECOND TIME

While everyone was marvelling at all that Jesus did, he said to his disciples, ⁴⁴'Listen carefully to what I am about to tell you: the Son of Man is going to be delivered into the hands of men.' ⁴⁵But they did not understand what this meant. It was hidden from them, so that they did not grasp it, and they were afraid to ask him about it.

⁴⁶An argument started among the disciples as to which of them would be the greatest. ⁴⁷Jesus, knowing their thoughts, took a little child and made him stand beside him. ⁴⁸Then he said to them, 'Whoever welcomes this little child in my name welcomes me; and whoever welcomes me welcomes the one who sent me. For it is the one who is least among you all who is the greatest.'

⁴⁹'Master,' said John, 'we saw someone driving out demons in your name and we tried to stop him, because he is not one of us.'

⁵⁰'Do not stop him,' Jesus said, 'for whoever is not against you is for you.'

SAMARITAN OPPOSITION

⁵¹As the time approached for him to be taken up to heaven, Jesus resolutely set out for Jerusalem. ⁵²And he sent messengers on ahead, who went into a Samaritan village to get things ready for him; ⁵³but the people there did not welcome him, because he was heading for Jerusalem. ⁵⁴When the disciples James and John saw this, they asked, 'Lord, do you want us to call fire down from heaven to destroy them?' ⁵⁵But Jesus turned and rebuked them. ⁵⁶Then he and his disciples went to another village.

THE COST OF FOLLOWING JESUS

⁵⁷As they were walking along the road, a man said to him, 'I will follow you wherever you go.'

⁵⁸Jesus replied, 'Foxes have dens and birds have nests, but the Son of Man has nowhere to lay his head.'

⁵⁹He said to another man, 'Follow me.'

But he replied, 'Lord, first let me go and bury my father.'

⁶⁰Jesus said to him, 'Let the dead bury their own dead, but you go and proclaim the kingdom of God.'

⁶¹Still another said, 'I will follow you, Lord; but first let me go back and say goodbye to my family.'

⁶²Jesus replied, 'No one who puts a hand to the plough and looks back is fit for service in the kingdom of God.'

JESUS SENDS OUT THE SEVENTY-TWO

10 After this the Lord appointed seventy-two others and sent them two by two ahead of him to every town and place where he was about to go. ²He told them, 'The harvest is plentiful, but the workers are few. Ask the Lord of the harvest, therefore, to send out workers into his harvest field. ³Go! I am sending you out like lambs among wolves. ⁴Do not take a purse or bag or sandals; and do not greet anyone on the road.

⁵'When you enter a house, first say, "Peace to this house." ⁶If someone who promotes peace is there, your peace will rest on them; if not, it will return to you. ⁷Stay there, eating and drinking whatever they give you, for the worker deserves his wages. Do not move around from house to house.

⁸'When you enter a town and are welcomed, eat what is offered to you. ⁹Heal those there who are ill and tell them, "The kingdom of God has come near to you." ¹⁰But when you enter a town and are not welcomed, go into its streets and say, ¹¹"Even the dust of your town we wipe from our feet as a warning to you. Yet be sure of this: the kingdom of God has come near." ¹²I tell you, it will be more bearable on that day for Sodom than for that town.

¹³'Woe to you, Chorazin! Woe to you, Bethsaida! For if the miracles that were performed in you had been performed in Tyre and Sidon, they would have repented long ago, sitting in sackcloth and ashes. ¹⁴But it will be more bearable for Tyre and Sidon at the judgment than for you. ¹⁵And you, Capernaum, will you be lifted to the heavens? No, you will go down to Hades.

¹⁶'Whoever listens to you listens to me; whoever rejects you rejects me; but whoever rejects me rejects him who sent me.'

¹⁷The seventy-two returned with joy and said, 'Lord, even the demons submit to us in your name.'

¹⁸He replied, 'I saw Satan fall like lightning from heaven. ¹⁹I have given you authority to trample on snakes and scorpions and to overcome all the power of the enemy; nothing will harm you. ²⁰However, do not rejoice that the spirits submit to you, but rejoice that your names are written in heaven.'

²¹At that time Jesus, full of joy through the Holy Spirit, said, 'I praise you, Father, Lord of heaven and earth, because you have hidden these things from the wise and learned, and revealed them to little children. Yes, Father, for this is what you were pleased to do.

²²'All things have been committed to me by my Father. No one knows who the Son is except the Father, and no one knows who the Father is except the Son and those to whom the Son chooses to reveal him.'

²³Then he turned to his disciples and said privately, 'Blessed are the eyes that see what you see. ²⁴For I tell you that many prophets

and kings wanted to see what you see but did not see it, and to hear what you hear but did not hear it.'

THE PARABLE OF THE GOOD SAMARITAN

25 On one occasion an expert in the law stood up to test Jesus. 'Teacher,' he asked, 'what must I do to inherit eternal life?'

26 'What is written in the Law?' he replied. 'How do you read it?'

27 He answered, '"Love the Lord your God with all your heart and with all your soul and with all your strength and with all your mind"; and, "Love your neighbour as yourself."'

28 'You have answered correctly,' Jesus replied. 'Do this and you will live.'

29 But he wanted to justify himself, so he asked Jesus, 'And who is my neighbour?'

30 In reply Jesus said: 'A man was going down from Jerusalem to Jericho, when he was attacked by robbers. They stripped him of his clothes, beat him and went away, leaving him half-dead. 31 A priest happened to be going down the same road, and when he saw the man, he passed by on the other side. 32 So too, a Levite, when he came to the place and saw him, passed by on the other side. 33 But a Samaritan, as he travelled, came where the man was; and when he saw him, he took pity on him. 34 He went to him and bandaged his wounds, pouring on oil and wine. Then he put the man on his own donkey, brought him to an inn and took care of him. 35 The next day he took out two denarii and gave them to the innkeeper. "Look after him," he said, "and when I return, I will reimburse you for any extra expense you may have."

36 'Which of these three do you think was a neighbour to the man who fell into the hands of robbers?'

37 The expert in the law replied, 'The one who had mercy on him.' Jesus told him, 'Go and do likewise.'

AT THE HOME OF MARTHA AND MARY

38 As Jesus and his disciples were on their way, he came to a village where a woman named Martha opened her home to him. 39 She had a sister called Mary, who sat at the Lord's feet listening to what he said. 40 But Martha was distracted by all the preparations that had to be made. She came to him and asked, 'Lord, don't you care that my sister has left me to do the work by myself? Tell her to help me!'

41 'Martha, Martha,' the Lord answered, 'you are worried and upset about many things, 42 but few things are needed – or indeed only one. Mary has chosen what is better, and it will not be taken away from her.'

JESUS' TEACHING ON PRAYER

11 One day Jesus was praying in a certain place. When he finished, one of his disciples said to him, 'Lord, teach us to pray, just as John taught his disciples.'

2 He said to them, 'When you pray, say:

' "Father,
    hallowed be your name,
    your kingdom come.
3 Give us each day our daily bread.
4 Forgive us our sins,
    for we also forgive everyone who sins against us.
And lead us not into temptation."'

5 Then Jesus said to them, 'Suppose you have a friend, and you go to him at midnight and say, "Friend, lend me three loaves of bread; 6 a friend of mine on a journey has come to me, and I have no food to offer him." 7 And suppose the one inside answers, "Don't bother me. The door is already locked, and my children and I are in bed. I can't get up and give you anything." 8 I tell you, even though he will not get up and give you the bread because of friendship, yet because of your shameless audacity he will surely get up and give you as much as you need.

9 'So I say to you: ask and it will be given to you; seek and you will find; knock and the door will be opened to you. 10 For everyone who asks receives; the one who seeks finds; and to the one who knocks, the door will be opened.

11 'Which of you fathers, if your son asks for a fish, will give him a snake instead? 12 Or if he asks for an egg, will give him a scorpion? 13 If you then, though you are evil, know how to give good gifts to your children, how much more will your Father in heaven give the Holy Spirit to those who ask him!'

JESUS AND BEELZEBUL

14 Jesus was driving out a demon that was mute. When the demon left, the man who had been mute spoke, and the crowd was amazed. 15 But some of them said, 'By Beelzebul, the prince of demons, he is driving out demons.' 16 Others tested him by asking for a sign from heaven.

17 Jesus knew their thoughts and said to them: 'Any kingdom divided against itself will be ruined, and a house divided against itself will fall. 18 If Satan is divided against himself, how can his kingdom stand? I say this because you claim that I drive out demons by Beelzebul. 19 Now if I drive out demons by Beelzebul, by whom do your followers drive them out? So then, they will be

your judges. **20**But if I drive out demons by the finger of God, then the kingdom of God has come upon you.

21'When a strong man, fully armed, guards his own house, his possessions are safe. **22**But when someone stronger attacks and overpowers him, he takes away the armour in which the man trusted and divides up his plunder.

23'Whoever is not with me is against me, and whoever does not gather with me scatters.

24'When an impure spirit comes out of a person, it goes through arid places seeking rest and does not find it. Then it says, "I will return to the house I left." **25**When it arrives, it finds the house swept clean and put in order. **26**Then it goes and takes seven other spirits more wicked than itself, and they go in and live there. And the final condition of that person is worse than the first.'

27As Jesus was saying these things, a woman in the crowd called out, 'Blessed is the mother who gave you birth and nursed you.'

28He replied, 'Blessed rather are those who hear the word of God and obey it.'

THE SIGN OF JONAH

29As the crowds increased, Jesus said, 'This is a wicked generation. It asks for a sign, but none will be given it except the sign of Jonah. **30**For as Jonah was a sign to the Ninevites, so also will the Son of Man be to this generation. **31**The Queen of the South will rise at the judgment with the people of this generation and condemn them, for she came from the ends of the earth to listen to Solomon's wisdom; and now something greater than Solomon is here. **32**The men of Nineveh will stand up at the judgment with this generation and condemn it, for they repented at the preaching of Jonah; and now something greater than Jonah is here.

THE LAMP OF THE BODY

33'No one lights a lamp and puts it in a place where it will be hidden, or under a bowl. Instead they put it on its stand, so that those who come in may see the light. **34**Your eye is the lamp of your body. When your eyes are healthy, your whole body also is full of light. But when they are unhealthy, your body also is full of darkness. **35**See to it, then, that the light within you is not darkness. **36**Therefore, if your whole body is full of light, and no part of it dark, it will be just as full of light as when a lamp shines its light on you.'

WOES ON THE PHARISEES AND THE EXPERTS IN THE LAW

37When Jesus had finished speaking, a Pharisee invited him to eat with him; so he went in and reclined at the table. **38**But the

Pharisee was surprised when he noticed that Jesus did not first wash before the meal.

39 Then the Lord said to him, 'Now then, you Pharisees clean the outside of the cup and dish, but inside you are full of greed and wickedness. **40** You foolish people! Did not the one who made the outside make the inside also? **41** But now as for what is inside you – be generous to the poor, and everything will be clean for you.

42 'Woe to you Pharisees, because you give God a tenth of your mint, rue and all other kinds of garden herbs, but you neglect justice and the love of God. You should have practised the latter without leaving the former undone.

43 'Woe to you Pharisees, because you love the most important seats in the synagogues and respectful greetings in the market-places.

44 'Woe to you, because you are like unmarked graves, which people walk over without knowing it.'

45 One of the experts in the law answered him, 'Teacher, when you say these things, you insult us also.'

46 Jesus replied, 'And you experts in the law, woe to you, because you load people down with burdens they can hardly carry, and you yourselves will not lift one finger to help them.

47 'Woe to you, because you build tombs for the prophets, and it was your ancestors who killed them. **48** So you testify that you approve of what your ancestors did; they killed the prophets, and you build their tombs. **49** Because of this, God in his wisdom said, "I will send them prophets and apostles, some of whom they will kill and others they will persecute." **50** Therefore this generation will be held responsible for the blood of all the prophets that has been shed since the beginning of the world, **51** from the blood of Abel to the blood of Zechariah, who was killed between the altar and the sanctuary. Yes, I tell you, this generation will be held responsible for it all.

52 'Woe to you experts in the law, because you have taken away the key to knowledge. You yourselves have not entered, and you have hindered those who were entering.'

53 When Jesus went outside, the Pharisees and the teachers of the law began to oppose him fiercely and to besiege him with questions, **54** waiting to catch him in something he might say.

WARNINGS AND ENCOURAGEMENTS

12 Meanwhile, when a crowd of many thousands had gathered, so that they were trampling on one another, Jesus began to speak first to his disciples, saying: 'Be on your guard against the yeast of the Pharisees, which is hypocrisy. **2** There is nothing concealed that will not be disclosed, or hidden that will not be made known. ³ What you have said in the dark will be heard in the daylight, and what you have whispered in the ear in the inner rooms will be proclaimed from the roofs.

⁴ 'I tell you, my friends, do not be afraid of those who kill the body and after that can do no more. ⁵ But I will show you whom you should fear: fear him who, after your body has been killed, has authority to throw you into hell. Yes, I tell you, fear him. ⁶ Are not five sparrows sold for two pennies? Yet not one of them is forgotten by God. ⁷ Indeed, the very hairs of your head are all numbered. Don't be afraid; you are worth more than many sparrows.

⁸ 'I tell you, whoever publicly acknowledges me before others, the Son of Man will also acknowledge before the angels of God. ⁹ But whoever disowns me before others will be disowned before the angels of God. ¹⁰ And everyone who speaks a word against the Son of Man will be forgiven, but anyone who blasphemes against the Holy Spirit will not be forgiven.

¹¹ 'When you are brought before synagogues, rulers and authorities, do not worry about how you will defend yourselves or what you will say, ¹² for the Holy Spirit will teach you at that time what you should say.'

THE PARABLE OF THE RICH FOOL

¹³ Someone in the crowd said to him, 'Teacher, tell my brother to divide the inheritance with me.'

¹⁴ Jesus replied, 'Man, who appointed me a judge or an arbiter between you?' ¹⁵ Then he said to them, 'Watch out! Be on your guard against all kinds of greed; life does not consist in an abundance of possessions.'

¹⁶ And he told them this parable: 'The ground of a certain rich man yielded an abundant harvest. ¹⁷ He thought to himself, "What shall I do? I have no place to store my crops."

¹⁸ 'Then he said, "This is what I'll do. I will tear down my barns and build bigger ones, and there I will store my surplus grain. ¹⁹ And I'll say to myself, 'You have plenty of grain laid up for many years. Take life easy; eat, drink and be merry.' "

²⁰ 'But God said to him, "You fool! This very night your life will be demanded from you. Then who will get what you have prepared for yourself?"

²¹ 'This is how it will be with whoever stores up things for themselves but is not rich towards God.'

DO NOT WORRY

²² Then Jesus said to his disciples: 'Therefore I tell you, do not worry about your life, what you will eat; or about your body, what you will wear. ²³ For life is more than food, and the body more than

clothes. 24 Consider the ravens: they do not sow or reap, they have no storeroom or barn; yet God feeds them. And how much more valuable you are than birds! 25 Who of you by worrying can add a single hour to your life? 26 Since you cannot do this very little thing, why do you worry about the rest?

27 'Consider how the wild flowers grow. They do not labour or spin. Yet I tell you, not even Solomon in all his splendour was dressed like one of these. 28 If that is how God clothes the grass of the field, which is here today, and tomorrow is thrown into the fire, how much more will he clothe you – you of little faith! 29 And do not set your heart on what you will eat or drink; do not worry about it. 30 For the pagan world runs after all such things, and your Father knows that you need them. 31 But seek his kingdom, and these things will be given to you as well.

32 'Do not be afraid, little flock, for your Father has been pleased to give you the kingdom. 33 Sell your possessions and give to the poor. Provide purses for yourselves that will not wear out, a treasure in heaven that will never fail, where no thief comes near and no moth destroys. 34 For where your treasure is, there your heart will be also.

WATCHFULNESS

35 'Be dressed ready for service and keep your lamps burning, 36 like servants waiting for their master to return from a wedding banquet, so that when he comes and knocks they can immediately open the door for him. 37 It will be good for those servants whose master finds them watching when he comes. Truly I tell you, he will dress himself to serve, will make them recline at the table and will come and wait on them. 38 It will be good for those servants whose master finds them ready, even if he comes in the middle of the night or towards daybreak. 39 But understand this: if the owner of the house had known at what hour the thief was coming, he would not have let his house be broken into. 40 You also must be ready, because the Son of Man will come at an hour when you do not expect him.'

41 Peter asked, 'Lord, are you telling this parable to us, or to everyone?'

42 The Lord answered, 'Who then is the faithful and wise manager, whom the master puts in charge of his servants to give them their food allowance at the proper time? 43 It will be good for that servant whom the master finds doing so when he returns. 44 Truly I tell you, he will put him in charge of all his possessions. 45 But suppose the servant says to himself, "My master is taking a long time in coming," and he then begins to beat the other servants, both men and women, and to eat and drink and get drunk. 46 The

master of that servant will come on a day when he does not expect him and at an hour he is not aware of. He will cut him to pieces and assign him a place with the unbelievers.

47'The servant who knows the master's will and does not get ready or does not do what the master wants will be beaten with many blows. 48But the one who does not know and does things deserving punishment will be beaten with few blows. From everyone who has been given much, much will be demanded; and from the one who has been entrusted with much, much more will be asked.

NOT PEACE BUT DIVISION

49'I have come to bring fire on the earth, and how I wish it were already kindled! 50But I have a baptism to undergo, and what constraint I am under until it is completed! 51Do you think I came to bring peace on earth? No, I tell you, but division. 52From now on there will be five in one family divided against each other, three against two and two against three. 53They will be divided, father against son and son against father, mother against daughter and daughter against mother, mother-in-law against daughter-in-law and daughter-in-law against mother-in-law.'

INTERPRETING THE TIMES

54He said to the crowd: 'When you see a cloud rising in the west, immediately you say, "It's going to rain," and it does. 55And when the south wind blows, you say, "It's going to be hot," and it is. 56Hypocrites! You know how to interpret the appearance of the earth and the sky. How is it that you don't know how to interpret this present time?

57'Why don't you judge for yourselves what is right? 58As you are going with your adversary to the magistrate, try hard to be reconciled on the way, or your adversary may drag you off to the judge, and the judge turn you over to the officer, and the officer throw you into prison. 59I tell you, you will not get out until you have paid the last penny.'

REPENT OR PERISH

13 Now there were some present at that time who told Jesus about the Galileans whose blood Pilate had mixed with their sacrifices. 2Jesus answered, 'Do you think that these Galileans were worse sinners than all the other Galileans because they suffered this way? 3I tell you, no! But unless you repent, you too will all perish. 4Or those eighteen who died when the tower in Siloam fell on them – do you think they were more guilty than all the others living in Jerusalem? 5I tell you, no! But unless you repent, you too will all perish.'

⁶Then he told this parable: 'A man had a fig-tree growing in his vineyard, and he went to look for fruit on it but did not find any. ⁷So he said to the man who took care of the vineyard, "For three years now I've been coming to look for fruit on this fig-tree and haven't found any. Cut it down! Why should it use up the soil?"

⁸'"Sir," the man replied, "leave it alone for one more year, and I'll dig round it and fertilise it. ⁹If it bears fruit next year, fine! If not, then cut it down."'

JESUS HEALS A CRIPPLED WOMAN ON THE SABBATH

¹⁰On a Sabbath Jesus was teaching in one of the synagogues, ¹¹and a woman was there who had been crippled by a spirit for eighteen years. She was bent over and could not straighten up at all. ¹²When Jesus saw her, he called her forward and said to her, 'Woman, you are set free from your infirmity.' ¹³Then he put his hands on her, and immediately she straightened up and praised God.

¹⁴Indignant because Jesus had healed on the Sabbath, the synagogue leader said to the people, 'There are six days for work. So come and be healed on those days, not on the Sabbath.'

¹⁵The Lord answered him, 'You hypocrites! Doesn't each of you on the Sabbath untie your ox or donkey from the stall and lead it out to give it water? ¹⁶Then should not this woman, a daughter of Abraham, whom Satan has kept bound for eighteen long years, be set free on the Sabbath day from what bound her?'

¹⁷When he said this, all his opponents were humiliated, but the people were delighted with all the wonderful things he was doing.

THE PARABLES OF THE MUSTARD SEED AND THE YEAST

¹⁸Then Jesus asked, 'What is the kingdom of God like? What shall I compare it to? ¹⁹It is like a mustard seed, which a man took and planted in his garden. It grew and became a tree, and the birds perched in its branches.'

²⁰Again he asked, 'What shall I compare the kingdom of God to? ²¹It is like yeast that a woman took and mixed into about thirty kilograms of flour until it worked all through the dough.'

THE NARROW DOOR

²²Then Jesus went through the towns and villages, teaching as he made his way to Jerusalem. ²³Someone asked him, 'Lord, are only a few people going to be saved?'

He said to them, ²⁴'Make every effort to enter through the narrow door, because many, I tell you, will try to enter and will not be able to. ²⁵Once the owner of the house gets up and closes the door, you will stand outside knocking and pleading, "Sir, open the door for us."

'But he will answer, "I don't know you or where you come from."
26 'Then you will say, "We ate and drank with you, and you taught in our streets."
27 'But he will reply, "I don't know you or where you come from. Away from me, all you evildoers!"
28 "There will be weeping there, and gnashing of teeth, when you see Abraham, Isaac and Jacob and all the prophets in the kingdom of God, but you yourselves thrown out. 29 People will come from east and west and north and south, and will take their places at the feast in the kingdom of God. 30 Indeed there are those who are last who will be first, and first who will be last.'

JESUS' SORROW FOR JERUSALEM

31 At that time some Pharisees came to Jesus and said to him, 'Leave this place and go somewhere else. Herod wants to kill you.'
32 He replied, 'Go and tell that fox, "I will keep on driving out demons and healing people today and tomorrow, and on the third day I will reach my goal." 33 In any case, I must press on today and tomorrow and the next day – for surely no prophet can die outside Jerusalem!
34 'Jerusalem, Jerusalem, you who kill the prophets and stone those sent to you, how often I have longed to gather your children together, as a hen gathers her chicks under her wings, and you were not willing. 35 Look, your house is left to you desolate. I tell you, you will not see me again until you say, "Blessed is he who comes in the name of the Lord."'

JESUS AT A PHARISEE'S HOUSE

14 One Sabbath, when Jesus went to eat in the house of a prominent Pharisee, he was being carefully watched. 2 There in front of him was a man suffering from abnormal swelling of his body. 3 Jesus asked the Pharisees and experts in the law, 'Is it lawful to heal on the Sabbath or not?' 4 But they remained silent. So taking hold of the man, he healed him and sent him on his way.
5 Then he asked them, 'If one of you has a child or an ox that falls into a well on the Sabbath day, will you not immediately pull it out?' 6 And they had nothing to say.
7 When he noticed how the guests picked the places of honour at the table, he told them this parable: 8 'When someone invites you to a wedding feast, do not take the place of honour, for a person more distinguished than you may have been invited. 9 If so, the host who invited both of you will come and say to you, "Give this person your seat." Then, humiliated, you will have to take the least important place. 10 But when you are invited, take the lowest place, so that when your host comes, he will say to you, "Friend, move

up to a better place." Then you will be honoured in the presence of all the other guests. ¹¹For all those who exalt themselves will be humbled, and those who humble themselves will be exalted.'

¹²Then Jesus said to his host, 'When you give a luncheon or dinner, do not invite your friends, your brothers or sisters, your relatives, or your rich neighbours; if you do, they may invite you back and so you will be repaid. ¹³But when you give a banquet, invite the poor, the crippled, the lame, the blind, ¹⁴and you will be blessed. Although they cannot repay you, you will be repaid at the resurrection of the righteous.'

THE PARABLE OF THE GREAT BANQUET

¹⁵When one of those at the table with him heard this, he said to Jesus, 'Blessed is the one who will eat at the feast in the kingdom of God.'

¹⁶Jesus replied: 'A certain man was preparing a great banquet and invited many guests. ¹⁷At the time of the banquet he sent his servant to tell those who had been invited, "Come, for everything is now ready."

¹⁸'But they all alike began to make excuses. The first said, "I have just bought a field, and I must go and see it. Please excuse me."

¹⁹'Another said, "I have just bought five yoke of oxen, and I'm on my way to try them out. Please excuse me."

²⁰'Still another said, "I have just got married, so I can't come."

²¹'The servant came back and reported this to his master. Then the owner of the house became angry and ordered his servant, "Go out quickly into the streets and alleys of the town and bring in the poor, the crippled, the blind and the lame."

²²' "Sir," the servant said, "what you ordered has been done, but there is still room."

²³'Then the master told his servant, "Go out to the roads and country lanes and compel them to come in, so that my house will be full. ²⁴I tell you, not one of those who were invited will get a taste of my banquet." '

THE COST OF BEING A DISCIPLE

²⁵Large crowds were travelling with Jesus, and turning to them he said: ²⁶'If anyone comes to me and does not hate father and mother, wife and children, brothers and sisters – yes, even their own life – such a person cannot be my disciple. ²⁷And whoever does not carry their cross and follow me cannot be my disciple.

²⁸'Suppose one of you wants to build a tower. Won't you first sit down and estimate the cost to see if you have enough money to complete it? ²⁹For if you lay the foundation and are not able to finish it, everyone who sees it will ridicule you, ³⁰saying, "This person began to build and wasn't able to finish."

31'Or suppose a king is about to go to war against another king. Won't he first sit down and consider whether he is able with ten thousand men to oppose the one coming against him with twenty thousand? 32If he is not able, he will send a delegation while the other is still a long way off and will ask for terms of peace. 33In the same way, those of you who do not give up everything you have cannot be my disciples.

34'Salt is good, but if it loses its saltiness, how can it be made salty again? 35It is fit neither for the soil nor for the manure heap; it is thrown out.

'Whoever has ears to hear, let them hear.'

THE PARABLE OF THE LOST SHEEP

15 Now the tax collectors and sinners were all gathering round to hear Jesus. 2But the Pharisees and the teachers of the law muttered, 'This man welcomes sinners, and eats with them.'

3Then Jesus told them this parable: 4'Suppose one of you has a hundred sheep and loses one of them. Doesn't he leave the ninety-nine in the open country and go after the lost sheep until he finds it? 5And when he finds it, he joyfully puts it on his shoulders 6and goes home. Then he calls his friends and neighbours together and says, "Rejoice with me; I have found my lost sheep." 7I tell you that in the same way there will be more rejoicing in heaven over one sinner who repents than over ninety-nine righteous people who do not need to repent.

THE PARABLE OF THE LOST COIN

8'Or suppose a woman has ten silver coins and loses one. Doesn't she light a lamp, sweep the house and search carefully until she finds it? 9And when she finds it, she calls her friends and neighbours together and says, "Rejoice with me; I have found my lost coin." 10In the same way, I tell you, there is rejoicing in the presence of the angels of God over one sinner who repents.'

THE PARABLE OF THE LOST SON

11Jesus continued: 'There was a man who had two sons. 12The younger one said to his father, "Father, give me my share of the estate." So he divided his property between them.

13'Not long after that, the younger son got together all he had, set off for a distant country and there squandered his wealth in wild living. 14After he had spent everything, there was a severe famine in that whole country, and he began to be in need. 15So he went and hired himself out to a citizen of that country, who sent him to his fields to feed pigs. 16He longed to fill his stomach with the pods that the pigs were eating, but no one gave him anything.

17'When he came to his senses, he said, "How many of my father's hired servants have food to spare, and here I am starving to death! 18I will set out and go back to my father and say to him: Father, I have sinned against heaven and against you. 19I am no longer worthy to be called your son; make me like one of your hired servants." 20So he got up and went to his father.

'But while he was still a long way off, his father saw him and was filled with compassion for him; he ran to his son, threw his arms round him and kissed him.

21'The son said to him, "Father, I have sinned against heaven and against you. I am no longer worthy to be called your son."

22'But the father said to his servants, "Quick! Bring the best robe and put it on him. Put a ring on his finger and sandals on his feet. 23Bring the fattened calf and kill it. Let's have a feast and celebrate. 24For this son of mine was dead and is alive again; he was lost and is found." So they began to celebrate.

25'Meanwhile, the elder son was in the field. When he came near the house, he heard music and dancing. 26So he called one of the servants and asked him what was going on. 27"Your brother has come," he replied, "and your father has killed the fattened calf because he has him back safe and sound."

28'The elder brother became angry and refused to go in. So his father went out and pleaded with him. 29But he answered his father, "Look! All these years I've been slaving for you and never disobeyed your orders. Yet you never gave me even a young goat so I could celebrate with my friends. 30But when this son of yours who has squandered your property with prostitutes comes home, you kill the fattened calf for him!"

31'"My son," the father said, "you are always with me, and everything I have is yours. 32But we had to celebrate and be glad, because this brother of yours was dead and is alive again; he was lost and is found."'

THE PARABLE OF THE SHREWD MANAGER

16 Jesus told his disciples: 'There was a rich man whose manager was accused of wasting his possessions. 2So he called him in and asked him, "What is this I hear about you? Give an account of your management, because you cannot be manager any longer."

3'The manager said to himself, "What shall I do now? My master is taking away my job. I'm not strong enough to dig, and I'm ashamed to beg – 4I know what I'll do so that, when I lose my job here, people will welcome me into their houses."

5'So he called in each one of his master's debtors. He asked the first, "How much do you owe my master?"

6 ' "Three thousand litres of olive oil," he replied.

'The manager told him, "Take your bill, sit down quickly, and make it fifteen hundred."

7 'Then he asked the second, "And how much do you owe?"

' "Thirty tons of wheat," he replied.

'He told him, "Take your bill and make it twenty-four."

8 'The master commended the dishonest manager because he had acted shrewdly. For the people of this world are more shrewd in dealing with their own kind than are the people of the light. **9** I tell you, use worldly wealth to gain friends for yourselves, so that when it is gone, you will be welcomed into eternal dwellings.

10 'Whoever can be trusted with very little can also be trusted with much, and whoever is dishonest with very little will also be dishonest with much. **11** So if you have not been trustworthy in handling worldly wealth, who will trust you with true riches? **12** And if you have not been trustworthy with someone else's property, who will give you property of your own?

13 'No one can serve two masters. Either you will hate the one and love the other, or you will be devoted to the one and despise the other. You cannot serve both God and Money.'

14 The Pharisees, who loved money, heard all this and were sneering at Jesus. **15** He said to them, 'You are the ones who justify yourselves in the eyes of others, but God knows your hearts. What people value highly is detestable in God's sight.

ADDITIONAL TEACHINGS

16 'The Law and the Prophets were proclaimed until John. Since that time, the good news of the kingdom of God is being preached, and everyone is forcing their way into it. **17** It is easier for heaven and earth to disappear than for the least stroke of a pen to drop out of the Law.

18 'Anyone who divorces his wife and marries another woman commits adultery, and the man who marries a divorced woman commits adultery.

THE RICH MAN AND LAZARUS

19 'There was a rich man who was dressed in purple and fine linen and lived in luxury every day. **20** At his gate was laid a beggar named Lazarus, covered with sores **21** and longing to eat what fell from the rich man's table. Even the dogs came and licked his sores.

22 'The time came when the beggar died and the angels carried him to Abraham's side. The rich man also died and was buried. **23** In Hades, where he was in torment, he looked up and saw Abraham far away, with Lazarus by his side. **24** So he called to him, "Father Abraham, have pity on me and send Lazarus to dip the tip of his finger in water and cool my tongue, because I am in agony in this fire."

25 'But Abraham replied, "Son, remember that in your lifetime you received your good things, while Lazarus received bad things, but now he is comforted here and you are in agony. **26** And besides all this, between us and you a great chasm has been set in place, so that those who want to go from here to you cannot, nor can anyone cross over from there to us."

27 'He answered, "Then I beg you, father, send Lazarus to my family, **28** for I have five brothers. Let him warn them, so that they will not also come to this place of torment."

29 'Abraham replied, "They have Moses and the Prophets; let them listen to them."

30 ' "No, father Abraham," he said, "but if someone from the dead goes to them, they will repent."

31 'He said to him, "If they do not listen to Moses and the Prophets, they will not be convinced even if someone rises from the dead." '

SIN, FAITH, DUTY

17 Jesus said to his disciples: 'Things that cause people to stumble are bound to come, but woe to anyone through whom they come. **2** It would be better for them to be thrown into the sea with a millstone tied round their neck than to cause one of these little ones to stumble. **3** So watch yourselves.

'If your brother or sister sins against you, rebuke them; and if they repent, forgive them. **4** Even if they sin against you seven times in a day and seven times come back to you saying "I repent," you must forgive them.'

5 The apostles said to the Lord, 'Increase our faith!'

6 He replied, 'If you have faith as small as a mustard seed, you can say to this mulberry tree, "Be uprooted and planted in the sea," and it will obey you.

7 'Suppose one of you has a servant ploughing or looking after the sheep. Will he say to the servant when he comes in from the field, "Come along now and sit down to eat"? **8** Won't he rather say, "Prepare my supper, get yourself ready and wait on me while I eat and drink; after that you may eat and drink"? **9** Will he thank the servant because he did what he was told to do? **10** So you also, when you have done everything you were told to do, should say, "We are unworthy servants; we have only done our duty." '

JESUS HEALS TEN MEN WITH LEPROSY

11 Now on his way to Jerusalem, Jesus travelled along the border between Samaria and Galilee. **12** As he was going into a village, ten men who had leprosy met him. They stood at a distance 13 and called out in a loud voice, 'Jesus, Master, have pity on us!'

14 When he saw them, he said, 'Go, show yourselves to the priests.' And as they went, they were cleansed.

15 One of them, when he saw he was healed, came back, praising God in a loud voice. 16 He threw himself at Jesus' feet and thanked him – and he was a Samaritan.

17 Jesus asked, 'Were not all ten cleansed? Where are the other nine? 18 Has no one returned to give praise to God except this foreigner?' 19 Then he said to him, 'Rise and go; your faith has made you well.'

THE COMING OF THE KINGDOM OF GOD

20 Once, on being asked by the Pharisees when the kingdom of God would come, Jesus replied, 'The coming of the kingdom of God is not something that can be observed, 21 nor will people say, "Here it is," or "There it is," because the kingdom of God is in your midst.'

22 Then he said to his disciples, 'The time is coming when you will long to see one of the days of the Son of Man, but you will not see it. 23 People will tell you, "There he is!" or "Here he is!" Do not go running off after them. 24 For the Son of Man in his day will be like the lightning, which flashes and lights up the sky from one end to the other. 25 But first he must suffer many things and be rejected by this generation.

26 'Just as it was in the days of Noah, so also will it be in the days of the Son of Man. 27 People were eating, drinking, marrying and being given in marriage up to the day Noah entered the ark. Then the flood came and destroyed them all.

28 'It was the same in the days of Lot. People were eating and drinking, buying and selling, planting and building. 29 But the day Lot left Sodom, fire and sulphur rained down from heaven and destroyed them all.

30 'It will be just like this on the day the Son of Man is revealed. 31 On that day no one who is on the housetop, with possessions inside, should go down to get them. Likewise, no one in the field should go back for anything. 32 Remember Lot's wife! 33 Whoever tries to keep their life will lose it, and whoever loses their life will preserve it. 34 I tell you, on that night two people will be in one bed; one will be taken and the other left. 35 Two women will be grinding corn together; one will be taken and the other left.' [36]a

37 'Where, Lord?' they asked.

He replied, 'Where there is a dead body, there the vultures will gather.'

a 36 *Some manuscripts include here words similar to Matt. 24:40.*

THE PARABLE OF THE PERSISTENT WIDOW

18 Then Jesus told his disciples a parable to show them that they should always pray and not give up. ²He said: 'In a certain town there was a judge who neither feared God nor cared what people thought. ³And there was a widow in that town who kept coming to him with the plea, "Grant me justice against my adversary."

⁴'For some time he refused. But finally he said to himself, "Even though I don't fear God or care what people think, ⁵yet because this widow keeps bothering me, I will see that she gets justice, so that she won't eventually come and attack me!"'

⁶And the Lord said, 'Listen to what the unjust judge says. ⁷And will not God bring about justice for his chosen ones, who cry out to him day and night? Will he keep putting them off? ⁸I tell you, he will see that they get justice, and quickly. However, when the Son of Man comes, will he find faith on the earth?'

THE PARABLE OF THE PHARISEE AND THE TAX COLLECTOR

⁹To some who were confident of their own righteousness and looked down on everyone else, Jesus told this parable: ¹⁰'Two men went up to the temple to pray, one a Pharisee and the other a tax collector. ¹¹The Pharisee stood by himself and prayed: "God, I thank you that I am not like other people – robbers, evildoers, adulterers – or even like this tax collector. ¹²I fast twice a week and give a tenth of all I get."

¹³'But the tax collector stood at a distance. He would not even look up to heaven, but beat his breast and said, "God, have mercy on me, a sinner."

¹⁴'I tell you that this man, rather than the other, went home justified before God. For all those who exalt themselves will be humbled, and those who humble themselves will be exalted.'

THE LITTLE CHILDREN AND JESUS

¹⁵People were also bringing babies to Jesus for him to place his hands on them. When the disciples saw this, they rebuked them. ¹⁶But Jesus called the children to him and said, 'Let the little children come to me, and do not hinder them, for the kingdom of God belongs to such as these. ¹⁷Truly I tell you, anyone who will not receive the kingdom of God like a little child will never enter it.'

THE RICH AND THE KINGDOM OF GOD

¹⁸A certain ruler asked him, 'Good teacher, what must I do to inherit eternal life?'

¹⁹'Why do you call me good?' Jesus answered. 'No one is good – except God alone. ²⁰You know the commandments: "You shall not

commit adultery, you shall not murder, you shall not steal, you shall not give false testimony, honour your father and mother."'

21 'All these I have kept since I was a boy,' he said.

22 When Jesus heard this, he said to him, 'You still lack one thing. Sell everything you have and give to the poor, and you will have treasure in heaven. Then come, follow me.'

23 When he heard this, he became very sad, because he was very wealthy. 24 Jesus looked at him and said, 'How hard it is for the rich to enter the kingdom of God! 25 Indeed, it is easier for a camel to go through the eye of a needle than for someone who is rich to enter the kingdom of God.'

26 Those who heard this asked, 'Who then can be saved?'

27 Jesus replied, 'What is impossible with man is possible with God.'

28 Peter said to him, 'We have left all we had to follow you!'

29 'Truly I tell you,' Jesus said to them, 'no one who has left home or wife or brothers or sisters or parents or children for the sake of the kingdom of God 30 will fail to receive many times as much in this age, and in the age to come eternal life.'

JESUS PREDICTS HIS DEATH A THIRD TIME

31 Jesus took the Twelve aside and told them, 'We are going up to Jerusalem, and everything that is written by the prophets about the Son of Man will be fulfilled. 32 He will be handed over to the Gentiles. They will mock him, insult him and spit on him; 33 they will flog him and kill him. On the third day he will rise again.'

34 The disciples did not understand any of this. Its meaning was hidden from them, and they did not know what he was talking about.

A BLIND BEGGAR RECEIVES HIS SIGHT

35 As Jesus approached Jericho, a blind man was sitting by the roadside begging. 36 When he heard the crowd going by, he asked what was happening. 37 They told him, 'Jesus of Nazareth is passing by.'

38 He called out, 'Jesus, Son of David, have mercy on me!'

39 Those who led the way rebuked him and told him to be quiet, but he shouted all the more, 'Son of David, have mercy on me!'

40 Jesus stopped and ordered the man to be brought to him. When he came near, Jesus asked him, 41 'What do you want me to do for you?'

'Lord, I want to see,' he replied.

42 Jesus said to him, 'Receive your sight; your faith has healed you.' 43 Immediately he received his sight and followed Jesus, praising God. When all the people saw it, they also praised God.

ZACCHAEUS THE TAX COLLECTOR

19 Jesus entered Jericho and was passing through. ²A man was there by the name of Zacchaeus; he was a chief tax collector and was wealthy. ³He wanted to see who Jesus was, but because he was short he could not see over the crowd. ⁴So he ran ahead and climbed a sycamore-fig tree to see him, since Jesus was coming that way.

⁵When Jesus reached the spot, he looked up and said to him, 'Zacchaeus, come down immediately. I must stay at your house today.' ⁶So he came down at once and welcomed him gladly.

⁷All the people saw this and began to mutter, 'He has gone to be the guest of a sinner.'

⁸But Zacchaeus stood up and said to the Lord, 'Look, Lord! Here and now I give half of my possessions to the poor, and if I have cheated anybody out of anything, I will pay back four times the amount.'

⁹Jesus said to him, 'Today salvation has come to this house, because this man, too, is a son of Abraham. ¹⁰For the Son of Man came to seek and to save the lost.'

THE PARABLE OF THE TEN MINAS

¹¹While they were listening to this, he went on to tell them a parable, because he was near Jerusalem and the people thought that the kingdom of God was going to appear at once. ¹²He said: 'A man of noble birth went to a distant country to have himself appointed king and then to return. ¹³So he called ten of his servants and gave them ten minas. "Put this money to work," he said, "until I come back."

¹⁴'But his subjects hated him and sent a delegation after him to say, "We don't want this man to be our king."

¹⁵'He was made king, however, and returned home. Then he sent for the servants to whom he had given the money, in order to find out what they had gained with it.

¹⁶'The first one came and said, "Sir, your mina has earned ten more."

¹⁷'"Well done, my good servant!" his master replied. "Because you have been trustworthy in a very small matter, take charge of ten cities."

¹⁸'The second came and said, "Sir, your mina has earned five more."

¹⁹'His master answered, "You take charge of five cities."

²⁰'Then another servant came and said, "Sir, here is your mina; I have kept it laid away in a piece of cloth. ²¹I was afraid of you, because you are a hard man. You take out what you did not put in and reap what you did not sow."

²²'His master replied, "I will judge you by your own words, you wicked servant! You knew, did you, that I am a hard man, taking out what I did not put in, and reaping what I did not sow? ²³Why then didn't you put my money on deposit, so that when I came back, I could have collected it with interest?"

²⁴'Then he said to those standing by, "Take his mina away from him and give it to the one who has ten minas."

²⁵'"Sir," they said, "he already has ten!"

²⁶'He replied, "I tell you that to everyone who has, more will be given, but as for the one who has nothing, even what they have will be taken away. ²⁷But those enemies of mine who did not want me to be king over them – bring them here and kill them in front of me."'

JESUS COMES TO JERUSALEM AS KING

²⁸After Jesus had said this, he went on ahead, going up to Jerusalem. ²⁹As he approached Bethphage and Bethany at the hill called the Mount of Olives, he sent two of his disciples, saying to them, ³⁰'Go to the village ahead of you, and as you enter it, you will find a colt tied there, which no one has ever ridden. Untie it and bring it here. ³¹If anyone asks you, "Why are you untying it?" say, "The Lord needs it."'

³²Those who were sent ahead went and found it just as he had told them. ³³As they were untying the colt, its owners asked them, 'Why are you untying the colt?'

³⁴They replied, 'The Lord needs it.'

³⁵They brought it to Jesus, threw their cloaks on the colt and put Jesus on it. ³⁶As he went along, people spread their cloaks on the road.

³⁷When he came near the place where the road goes down the Mount of Olives, the whole crowd of disciples began joyfully to praise God in loud voices for all the miracles they had seen:

³⁸'Blessed is the king who comes in the name of the Lord!'

'Peace in heaven and glory in the highest!'

³⁹Some of the Pharisees in the crowd said to Jesus, 'Teacher, rebuke your disciples!'

⁴⁰'I tell you,' he replied, 'if they keep quiet, the stones will cry out.'

⁴¹As he approached Jerusalem and saw the city, he wept over it ⁴²and said, 'If you, even you, had only known on this day what would bring you peace – but now it is hidden from your eyes. ⁴³The days will come upon you when your enemies will build an embankment against you and encircle you and hem you in on

every side. **44** They will dash you to the ground, you and the children within your walls. They will not leave one stone on another, because you did not recognise the time of God's coming to you.'

JESUS AT THE TEMPLE

45 When Jesus entered the temple courts, he began to drive out those who were selling. **46** 'It is written,' he said to them, ' "My house will be a house of prayer"; but you have made it "a den of robbers".'

47 Every day he was teaching at the temple. But the chief priests, the teachers of the law and the leaders among the people were trying to kill him. **48** Yet they could not find any way to do it, because all the people hung on his words.

THE AUTHORITY OF JESUS QUESTIONED

20 One day as Jesus was teaching the people in the temple courts and proclaiming the good news, the chief priests and the teachers of the law, together with the elders, came up to him. **2** 'Tell us by what authority you are doing these things,' they said. 'Who gave you this authority?'

3 He replied, 'I will also ask you a question. Tell me: **4** John's baptism – was it from heaven, or of human origin?'

5 They discussed it among themselves and said, 'If we say, "From heaven," he will ask, "Why didn't you believe him?" **6** But if we say, "Of human origin," all the people will stone us, because they are persuaded that John was a prophet.'

7 So they answered, 'We don't know where it was from.'

8 Jesus said, 'Neither will I tell you by what authority I am doing these things.'

THE PARABLE OF THE TENANTS

9 He went on to tell the people this parable: 'A man planted a vineyard, rented it to some farmers and went away for a long time. **10** At harvest time he sent a servant to the tenants so they would give him some of the fruit of the vineyard. But the tenants beat him and sent him away empty-handed. **11** He sent another servant, but that one also they beat and treated shamefully and sent away empty-handed. **12** He sent still a third, and they wounded him and threw him out.

13 'Then the owner of the vineyard said, "What shall I do? I will send my son, whom I love; perhaps they will respect him."

14 'But when the tenants saw him, they talked the matter over. "This is the heir," they said. "Let's kill him, and the inheritance will be ours." **15** So they threw him out of the vineyard and killed him.

'What then will the owner of the vineyard do to them? **16** He will come and kill those tenants and give the vineyard to others.'

When the people heard this, they said, 'God forbid!'

17 Jesus looked directly at them and asked, 'Then what is the meaning of that which is written:

' "The stone the builders rejected
has become the cornerstone"?

18 Everyone who falls on that stone will be broken to pieces; anyone on whom it falls will be crushed.'

19 The teachers of the law and the chief priests looked for a way to arrest him immediately, because they knew he had spoken this parable against them. But they were afraid of the people.

PAYING TAXES TO CAESAR

20 Keeping a close watch on him, they sent spies, who pretended to be sincere. They hoped to catch Jesus in something he said, so that they might hand him over to the power and authority of the governor. 21 So the spies questioned him: 'Teacher, we know that you speak and teach what is right, and that you do not show partiality but teach the way of God in accordance with the truth. 22 Is it right for us to pay taxes to Caesar or not?'

23 He saw through their duplicity and said to them, 24 'Show me a denarius. Whose image and inscription are on it?'

'Caesar's,' they replied.

25 He said to them, 'Then give back to Caesar what is Caesar's, and to God what is God's.'

26 They were unable to trap him in what he had said there in public. And astonished by his answer, they became silent.

THE RESURRECTION AND MARRIAGE

27 Some of the Sadducees, who say there is no resurrection, came to Jesus with a question. 28 'Teacher,' they said, 'Moses wrote for us that if a man's brother dies and leaves a wife but no children, the man must marry the widow and raise up offspring for his brother. 29 Now there were seven brothers. The first one married a woman and died childless. 30 The second 31 and then the third married her, and in the same way the seven died, leaving no children. 32 Finally, the woman died too. 33 Now then, at the resurrection whose wife will she be, since the seven were married to her?'

34 Jesus replied, 'The people of this age marry and are given in marriage. 35 But those who are considered worthy of taking part in the age to come and in the resurrection from the dead will neither marry nor be given in marriage, 36 and they can no longer die; for they are like the angels. They are God's children, since they are children of the resurrection. 37 But in the account of the burning bush, even Moses showed that the dead rise, for he calls the

Lord "the God of Abraham, and the God of Isaac, and the God of Jacob". ³⁸He is not the God of the dead, but of the living, for to him all are alive.'

³⁹Some of the teachers of the law responded, 'Well said, teacher!' ⁴⁰And no one dared to ask him any more questions.

WHOSE SON IS THE MESSIAH?

⁴¹Then Jesus said to them, 'Why is it said that the Messiah is the son of David? ⁴²David himself declares in the Book of Psalms:

' "The Lord said to my Lord:
    'Sit at my right hand
⁴³ until I make your enemies
    a footstool for your feet.' "

⁴⁴David calls him "Lord." How then can he be his son?'

WARNING AGAINST THE TEACHERS OF THE LAW

⁴⁵While all the people were listening, Jesus said to his disciples, ⁴⁶'Beware of the teachers of the law. They like to walk around in flowing robes and love to be greeted with respect in the market-places and have the most important seats in the synagogues and the places of honour at banquets. ⁴⁷They devour widows' houses and for a show make lengthy prayers. These men will be punished most severely.'

THE WIDOW'S OFFERING

21 As Jesus looked up, he saw the rich putting their gifts into the temple treasury. ²He also saw a poor widow put in two very small copper coins. ³'Truly I tell you,' he said, 'this poor widow has put in more than all the others. ⁴All these people gave their gifts out of their wealth; but she out of her poverty put in all she had to live on.'

THE DESTRUCTION OF THE TEMPLE AND SIGNS OF THE END TIMES

⁵Some of his disciples were remarking about how the temple was adorned with beautiful stones and with gifts dedicated to God. But Jesus said, ⁶'As for what you see here, the time will come when not one stone will be left on another; every one of them will be thrown down.'

⁷'Teacher,' they asked, 'when will these things happen? And what will be the sign that they are about to take place?'

⁸He replied: 'Watch out that you are not deceived. For many will come in my name, claiming, "I am he," and, "The time is near." Do not follow them. ⁹When you hear of wars and uprisings, do

not be frightened. These things must happen first, but the end will not come right away.'

10 Then he said to them: 'Nation will rise against nation, and kingdom against kingdom. 11 There will be great earthquakes, famines and pestilences in various places, and fearful events and great signs from heaven.

12 'But before all this, they will seize you and persecute you. They will hand you over to synagogues and put you in prison, and you will be brought before kings and governors, and all on account of my name. 13 And so you will bear testimony to me. 14 But make up your mind not to worry beforehand how you will defend yourselves. 15 For I will give you words and wisdom that none of your adversaries will be able to resist or contradict. 16 You will be betrayed even by parents, brothers and sisters, relatives and friends, and they will put some of you to death. 17 Everyone will hate you because of me. 18 But not a hair of your head will perish. 19 Stand firm, and you will win life.

20 'When you see Jerusalem being surrounded by armies, you will know that its desolation is near. 21 Then let those who are in Judea flee to the mountains, let those in the city get out, and let those in the country not enter the city. 22 For this is the time of punishment in fulfilment of all that has been written. 23 How dreadful it will be in those days for pregnant women and nursing mothers! There will be great distress in the land and wrath against this people. 24 They will fall by the sword and will be taken as prisoners to all the nations. Jerusalem will be trampled on by the Gentiles until the times of the Gentiles are fulfilled.

25 'There will be signs in the sun, moon and stars. On the earth, nations will be in anguish and perplexity at the roaring and tossing of the sea. 26 People will faint from terror, apprehensive of what is coming on the world, for the heavenly bodies will be shaken. 27 At that time they will see the Son of Man coming in a cloud with power and great glory. 28 When these things begin to take place, stand up and lift up your heads, because your redemption is drawing near.'

29 He told them this parable: 'Look at the fig-tree and all the trees. 30 When they sprout leaves, you can see for yourselves and know that summer is near. 31 Even so, when you see these things happening, you know that the kingdom of God is near.

32 'Truly I tell you, this generation will certainly not pass away until all these things have happened. 33 Heaven and earth will pass away, but my words will never pass away.

34 'Be careful, or your hearts will be weighed down with carousing, drunkenness and the anxieties of life, and that day will close on you suddenly like a trap. 35 For it will come on all those who live

on the face of the whole earth. ³⁶Be always on the watch, and pray that you may be able to escape all that is about to happen, and that you may be able to stand before the Son of Man.'

³⁷Each day Jesus was teaching at the temple, and each evening he went out to spend the night on the hill called the Mount of Olives, ³⁸and all the people came early in the morning to hear him at the temple.

JUDAS AGREES TO BETRAY JESUS

22 Now the Festival of Unleavened Bread, called the Passover, was approaching, ²and the chief priests and the teachers of the law were looking for some way to get rid of Jesus, for they were afraid of the people. ³Then Satan entered Judas, called Iscariot, one of the Twelve. ⁴And Judas went to the chief priests and the officers of the temple guard and discussed with them how he might betray Jesus. ⁵They were delighted and agreed to give him money. ⁶He consented, and watched for an opportunity to hand Jesus over to them when no crowd was present.

THE LAST SUPPER

⁷Then came the day of Unleavened Bread on which the Passover lamb had to be sacrificed. ⁸Jesus sent Peter and John, saying, 'Go and make preparations for us to eat the Passover.'

⁹'Where do you want us to prepare for it?' they asked.

¹⁰He replied, 'As you enter the city, a man carrying a jar of water will meet you. Follow him to the house that he enters, ¹¹and say to the owner of the house, "The Teacher asks: where is the guest room, where I may eat the Passover with my disciples?" ¹²He will show you a large room upstairs, all furnished. Make preparations there.'

¹³They left and found things just as Jesus had told them. So they prepared the Passover.

¹⁴When the hour came, Jesus and his apostles reclined at the table. ¹⁵And he said to them, 'I have eagerly desired to eat this Passover with you before I suffer. ¹⁶For I tell you, I will not eat it again until it finds fulfilment in the kingdom of God.'

¹⁷After taking the cup, he gave thanks and said, 'Take this and divide it among you. ¹⁸For I tell you I will not drink again from the fruit of the vine until the kingdom of God comes.'

¹⁹And he took bread, gave thanks and broke it, and gave it to them, saying, 'This is my body given for you; do this in remembrance of me.'

²⁰In the same way, after the supper he took the cup, saying, 'This cup is the new covenant in my blood, which is poured out for you. ²¹But the hand of him who is going to betray me is with mine on the table. ²²The Son of Man will go as it has been decreed.

But woe to that man who betrays him!' **23**They began to question among themselves which of them it might be who would do this.

24A dispute also arose among them as to which of them was considered to be greatest. **25**Jesus said to them, 'The kings of the Gentiles lord it over them; and those who exercise authority over them call themselves Benefactors. **26**But you are not to be like that. Instead, the greatest among you should be like the youngest, and the one who rules like the one who serves. **27**For who is greater, the one who is at the table or the one who serves? Is it not the one who is at the table? But I am among you as one who serves. **28**You are those who have stood by me in my trials. **29**And I confer on you a kingdom, just as my Father conferred one on me, **30**so that you may eat and drink at my table in my kingdom and sit on thrones, judging the twelve tribes of Israel.

31'Simon, Simon, Satan has asked to sift all of you as wheat. **32**But I have prayed for you, Simon, that your faith may not fail. And when you have turned back, strengthen your brothers.'

33But he replied, 'Lord, I am ready to go with you to prison and to death.'

34Jesus answered, 'I tell you, Peter, before the cock crows today, you will deny three times that you know me.'

35Then Jesus asked them, 'When I sent you without purse, bag or sandals, did you lack anything?'

'Nothing,' they answered.

36He said to them, 'But now if you have a purse, take it, and also a bag; and if you don't have a sword, sell your cloak and buy one. **37**It is written: "And he was numbered with the transgressors"; and I tell you that this must be fulfilled in me. Yes, what is written about me is reaching its fulfilment.'

38The disciples said, 'See, Lord, here are two swords.'

'That's enough!' he replied.

JESUS PRAYS ON THE MOUNT OF OLIVES

39Jesus went out as usual to the Mount of Olives, and his disciples followed him. **40**On reaching the place, he said to them, 'Pray that you will not fall into temptation.' **41**He withdrew about a stone's throw beyond them, knelt down and prayed, **42**'Father, if you are willing, take this cup from me; yet not my will, but yours be done.' **43**An angel from heaven appeared to him and strengthened him. **44**And being in anguish, he prayed more earnestly, and his sweat was like drops of blood falling to the ground.

45When he rose from prayer and went back to the disciples, he found them asleep, exhausted from sorrow. **46**'Why are you sleeping?' he asked them. 'Get up and pray so that you will not fall into temptation.'

JESUS ARRESTED

47 While he was still speaking a crowd came up, and the man who was called Judas, one of the Twelve, was leading them. He approached Jesus to kiss him, **48** but Jesus asked him, 'Judas, are you betraying the Son of Man with a kiss?'

49 When Jesus' followers saw what was going to happen, they said, 'Lord, should we strike with our swords?' **50** And one of them struck the servant of the high priest, cutting off his right ear.

51 But Jesus answered, 'No more of this!' And he touched the man's ear and healed him.

52 Then Jesus said to the chief priests, the officers of the temple guard, and the elders, who had come for him, 'Am I leading a rebellion, that you have come with swords and clubs? **53** Every day I was with you in the temple courts, and you did not lay a hand on me. But this is your hour – when darkness reigns.'

PETER DISOWNS JESUS

54 Then seizing him, they led him away and took him into the house of the high priest. Peter followed at a distance. **55** And when some there had kindled a fire in the middle of the courtyard and had sat down together, Peter sat down with them. **56** A servant-girl saw him seated there in the firelight. She looked closely at him and said, 'This man was with him.'

57 But he denied it. 'Woman, I don't know him,' he said.

58 A little later someone else saw him and said, 'You also are one of them.'

'Man, I am not!' Peter replied.

59 About an hour later another asserted, 'Certainly this fellow was with him, for he is a Galilean.'

60 Peter replied, 'Man, I don't know what you're talking about!' Just as he was speaking, the cock crowed. **61** The Lord turned and looked straight at Peter. Then Peter remembered the word the Lord had spoken to him: 'Before the cock crows today, you will disown me three times.' **62** And he went outside and wept bitterly.

THE GUARDS MOCK JESUS

63 The men who were guarding Jesus began mocking and beating him. **64** They blindfolded him and demanded, 'Prophesy! Who hit you?' **65** And they said many other insulting things to him.

JESUS BEFORE PILATE AND HEROD

66 At daybreak the council of the elders of the people, both the chief priests and the teachers of the law, met together, and Jesus was led before them. **67** 'If you are the Messiah,' they said, 'tell us.'

Jesus answered, 'If I tell you, you will not believe me, **68** and if I asked you, you would not answer. **69**But from now on, the Son of Man will be seated at the right hand of the mighty God.'

70They all asked, 'Are you then the Son of God?'

He replied, 'You say that I am.'

71Then they said, 'Why do we need any more testimony? We have heard it from his own lips.'

23 Then the whole assembly rose and led him off to Pilate. **2**And they began to accuse him, saying, 'We have found this man subverting our nation. He opposes payment of taxes to Caesar and claims to be Messiah, a king.'

3So Pilate asked Jesus, 'Are you the king of the Jews?'

'You have said so,' Jesus replied.

4Then Pilate announced to the chief priests and the crowd, 'I find no basis for a charge against this man.'

5But they insisted, 'He stirs up the people all over Judea by his teaching. He started in Galilee and has come all the way here.'

6On hearing this, Pilate asked if the man was a Galilean. **7**When he learned that Jesus was under Herod's jurisdiction, he sent him to Herod, who was also in Jerusalem at that time.

8When Herod saw Jesus, he was greatly pleased, because for a long time he had been wanting to see him. From what he had heard about him, he hoped to see him perform a sign of some sort. **9**He plied him with many questions, but Jesus gave him no answer. **10**The chief priests and the teachers of the law were standing there, vehemently accusing him. **11**Then Herod and his soldiers ridiculed and mocked him. Dressing him in an elegant robe, they sent him back to Pilate. **12**That day Herod and Pilate became friends – before this they had been enemies.

13Pilate called together the chief priests, the rulers and the people, **14**and said to them, 'You brought me this man as one who was inciting the people to rebellion. I have examined him in your presence and have found no basis for your charges against him. **15**Neither has Herod, for he sent him back to us; as you can see, he has done nothing to deserve death. **16**Therefore, I will punish him and then release him.' **[17]**a

18But the whole crowd shouted, 'Away with this man! Release Barabbas to us!' **19**(Barabbas had been thrown into prison for an insurrection in the city, and for murder.)

20Wanting to release Jesus, Pilate appealed to them again. **21**But they kept shouting, 'Crucify him! Crucify him!'

22For the third time he spoke to them: 'Why? What crime has this man committed? I have found in him no grounds for the death penalty. Therefore I will have him punished and then release him.'

23But with loud shouts they insistently demanded that he be

a 17 *Some manuscripts include here words similar to Matt. 27:15 and Mark 15:6.*

crucified, and their shouts prevailed. 24 So Pilate decided to grant their demand. 25 He released the man who had been thrown into prison for insurrection and murder, the one they asked for, and surrendered Jesus to their will.

THE CRUCIFIXION OF JESUS

26 As the soldiers led him away, they seized Simon from Cyrene, who was on his way in from the country, and put the cross on him and made him carry it behind Jesus. 27 A large number of people followed him, including women who mourned and wailed for him. 28 Jesus turned and said to them, 'Daughters of Jerusalem, do not weep for me; weep for yourselves and for your children. 29 For the time will come when you will say, "Blessed are the childless women, the wombs that never bore and the breasts that never nursed!" 30 Then

' "they will say to the mountains, 'Fall on us!'
    and to the hills, 'Cover us!' "

31 For if people do these things when the tree is green, what will happen when it is dry?'

32 Two other men, both criminals, were also led out with him to be executed. 33 When they came to the place called the Skull, they crucified him there, along with the criminals – one on his right, the other on his left. 34 Jesus said, 'Father, forgive them, for they do not know what they are doing.' And they divided up his clothes by casting lots.

35 The people stood watching, and the rulers even sneered at him. They said, 'He saved others; let him save himself if he is God's Messiah, the Chosen One.'

36 The soldiers also came up and mocked him. They offered him wine vinegar 37 and said, 'If you are the king of the Jews, save yourself.'

38 There was a written notice above him, which read: THIS IS THE KING OF THE JEWS.

39 One of the criminals who hung there hurled insults at him: 'Aren't you the Messiah? Save yourself and us!'

40 But the other criminal rebuked him. 'Don't you fear God,' he said, 'since you are under the same sentence? 41 We are punished justly, for we are getting what our deeds deserve. But this man has done nothing wrong.'

42 Then he said, 'Jesus, remember me when you come into your kingdom.'

43 Jesus answered him, 'Truly I tell you, today you will be with me in paradise.'

THE DEATH OF JESUS

44 It was now about noon, and darkness came over the whole land until three in the afternoon, 45 for the sun stopped shining. And the curtain of the temple was torn in two. 46 Jesus called out with a loud voice, 'Father, into your hands I commit my spirit.' When he had said this, he breathed his last.

47 The centurion, seeing what had happened, praised God and said, 'Surely this was a righteous man.' 48 When all the people who had gathered to witness this sight saw what took place, they beat their breasts and went away. 49 But all those who knew him, including the women who had followed him from Galilee, stood at a distance, watching these things.

THE BURIAL OF JESUS

50 Now there was a man named Joseph, a member of the Council, a good and upright man, 51 who had not consented to their decision and action. He came from the Judean town of Arimathea, and he himself was waiting for the kingdom of God. 52 Going to Pilate, he asked for Jesus' body. 53 Then he took it down, wrapped it in linen cloth and placed it in a tomb cut in the rock, one in which no one had yet been laid. 54 It was Preparation Day, and the Sabbath was about to begin.

55 The women who had come with Jesus from Galilee followed Joseph and saw the tomb and how his body was laid in it. 56 Then they went home and prepared spices and perfumes. But they rested on the Sabbath in obedience to the commandment.

JESUS HAS RISEN

24 On the first day of the week, very early in the morning, the women took the spices they had prepared and went to the tomb. 2 They found the stone rolled away from the tomb, 3 but when they entered, they did not find the body of the Lord Jesus. 4 While they were wondering about this, suddenly two men in clothes that gleamed like lightning stood beside them. 5 In their fright the women bowed down with their faces to the ground, but the men said to them, 'Why do you look for the living among the dead? 6 He is not here; he has risen! Remember how he told you, while he was still with you in Galilee: 7 "The Son of Man must be delivered over to the hands of sinners, be crucified and on the third day be raised again." ' 8 Then they remembered his words.

9 When they came back from the tomb, they told all these things to the Eleven and to all the others. 10 It was Mary Magdalene, Joanna, Mary the mother of James, and the others with them who told this to the apostles. 11 But they did not believe the women, because their words seemed to them like nonsense.

¹²Peter, however, got up and ran to the tomb. Bending over, he saw the strips of linen lying by themselves, and he went away, wondering to himself what had happened.

ON THE ROAD TO EMMAUS

¹³Now that same day two of them were going to a village called Emmaus, about seven miles from Jerusalem. ¹⁴They were talking with each other about everything that had happened. ¹⁵As they talked and discussed these things with each other, Jesus himself came up and walked along with them; ¹⁶but they were kept from recognising him.

¹⁷He asked them, 'What are you discussing together as you walk along?'

They stood still, their faces downcast. ¹⁸One of them, named Cleopas, asked him, 'Are you the only one visiting Jerusalem who does not know the things that have happened there in these days?'

¹⁹'What things?' he asked.

'About Jesus of Nazareth,' they replied. 'He was a prophet, powerful in word and deed before God and all the people. ²⁰The chief priests and our rulers handed him over to be sentenced to death, and they crucified him; ²¹but we had hoped that he was the one who was going to redeem Israel. And what is more, it is the third day since all this took place. ²²In addition, some of our women amazed us. They went to the tomb early this morning ²³but didn't find his body. They came and told us that they had seen a vision of angels, who said he was alive. ²⁴Then some of our companions went to the tomb and found it just as the women had said, but they did not see Jesus.'

²⁵He said to them, 'How foolish you are, and how slow to believe all that the prophets have spoken! ²⁶Did not the Messiah have to suffer these things and then enter his glory?' ²⁷And beginning with Moses and all the Prophets, he explained to them what was said in all the Scriptures concerning himself.

²⁸As they approached the village to which they were going, Jesus continued on as if he were going further. ²⁹But they urged him strongly, 'Stay with us, for it is nearly evening; the day is almost over.' So he went in to stay with them.

³⁰When he was at the table with them, he took bread, gave thanks, broke it and began to give it to them. ³¹Then their eyes were opened and they recognised him, and he disappeared from their sight. ³²They asked each other, 'Were not our hearts burning within us while he talked with us on the road and opened the Scriptures to us?'

³³They got up and returned at once to Jerusalem. There they found the Eleven and those with them, assembled together ³⁴and

saying, 'It is true! The Lord has risen and has appeared to Simon.'
³⁵Then the two told what had happened on the way, and how Jesus was recognised by them when he broke the bread.

JESUS APPEARS TO THE DISCIPLES

³⁶While they were still talking about this, Jesus himself stood among them and said to them, 'Peace be with you.'

³⁷They were startled and frightened, thinking they saw a ghost. ³⁸He said to them, 'Why are you troubled, and why do doubts rise in your minds? ³⁹Look at my hands and my feet. It is I myself! Touch me and see; a ghost does not have flesh and bones, as you see I have.'

⁴⁰When he had said this, he showed them his hands and feet. ⁴¹And while they still did not believe it because of joy and amazement, he asked them, 'Do you have anything here to eat?' ⁴²They gave him a piece of broiled fish, ⁴³and he took it and ate it in their presence.

⁴⁴He said to them, 'This is what I told you while I was still with you: everything must be fulfilled that is written about me in the Law of Moses, the Prophets and the Psalms.'

⁴⁵Then he opened their minds so they could understand the Scriptures. ⁴⁶He told them, 'This is what is written: the Messiah will suffer and rise from the dead on the third day, ⁴⁷and repentance for the forgiveness of sins will be preached in his name to all nations, beginning at Jerusalem. ⁴⁸You are witnesses of these things. ⁴⁹I am going to send you what my Father has promised; but stay in the city until you have been clothed with power from on high.'

THE ASCENSION OF JESUS

⁵⁰When he had led them out to the vicinity of Bethany, he lifted up his hands and blessed them. ⁵¹While he was blessing them, he left them and was taken up into heaven. ⁵²Then they worshipped him and returned to Jerusalem with great joy. ⁵³And they stayed continually at the temple, praising God.

Ernst van Dyk
SOUTH AFRICA

To compete in the Paralympics once is an impressive achievement. For Ernst van Dyk, however, 2012 marked his sixth Paralympics. Incredibly, the South African has represented his country in not one but three sports over the years.

Ernst was born with a congenital birth defect which, he explains, "means that somewhere along the line a switch did not flip and my legs did not grow. So from my knees down I have no legs and my right arm is a bit affected."

He started his Paralympic career as a swimmer in 1992 – the first Paralympics to which South Africa was admitted after the apartheid ban. The 19-year-old Ernst competed as a swimmer and an athlete. He took fifth place in the pool, but changed his career to track events after reaching the semifinals in the wheelchair events. Known for winning nine consecutive Boston Marathons (one of the world's most prestigious wheelchair marathons), in recent years Ernst's career has also encompassed handcycling.

It was a case of third time lucky for Ernst in Sydney in 2000, his third Paralympics, when he finally won a medal; bronze in the 400 metres. He also finished fourth in the marathon. In 2004, in Athens, he had his best Paralympics so far with two silver medals (800 and 1,500 metres) and a bronze medal in the 5,000 metres, as well as placing fifth in the 400 metres.

In Beijing in 2008 he came fourth in the men's individual handcycling time trial but picked up gold in the men's individual road race. He recalls the thrilling finish, "I broke away early in the race and was on my own for most of the race. There were two Americans, Alejandro Albor and Oz Sanchez, working together to close me down and with about 1km to go, the two Americans closed up on me and we went into the finish area together, but I was able to outsprint them and win the gold medal." He won in a time of 1 hour 21 minutes 40 seconds, just a second ahead of his two rivals. He also took bronze in the marathon at Beijing.

His sporting achievements are important to Ernst, but so is his faith. "I am a Christian. When you have been dealt the cards I have been dealt in life, you have to make sense

"You have to figure out what is your purpose in life."

of it. Faith is one of the ways to do that and to reach an understanding with your maker and to figure out what is your purpose in life."

The life of an athlete can be lonely, spending long hours training and travelling, and it can be hard to cope with the pressure. Ernst finds his Christian faith comforting when he worries that it may all be getting too much for him. "I travel a lot and I am

"When things get too much for you or you feel alone, it is so easy to talk to him."

on the road a lot and am alone a lot. Having Jesus is like having a friend on the road with me. When things get too much for you or you feel alone or get down because you are not getting the results, it is so easy to talk to him and be there and get guidance and feel the warmth."

He hopes that his faith and his achievements are also an inspiration to others. He says, "I was given a disability to overcome it and that was part of my process of growing up and how the Lord wanted to teach me to be a better person. I realised he had given me a talent. And the talent is to perform well on the world scene and to inspire people and to make people realise that when they think there is no way out, that there is actually a way out."

Dieudonné Disi
RWANDA

For any athlete, the chance to compete in the Olympic Games is an incredible achievement. But for Dieudonné Disi, reaching the Olympics was nothing short of miraculous given the obstacles he had already had to overcome in his life.

Born in Rwanda, Dieudonné's world changed forever one day in 1994, at the height of the genocide. Knowing that the rebels were coming, Dieudonné's father called him and his brothers together, telling them, "We are all going to die today. Let us pray and prepare to go to heaven." While the family prayed, Dieudonné went outside and hid. This saved his life. When his parents, siblings and all their neighbours were murdered minutes later, only Dieudonné escaped. He recalls, "I lay down in my father's garden and waited for night.

It was perhaps 7pm when I set off through the forest to the neighbouring country of Burundi. I had never been to Burundi in my life but I knew the direction. It was about 15 miles from my home." He was just fourteen.

When Dieudonné returned to Rwanda he joined the army, and he vividly remembers following the 1996 Olympics on the radio – he had no television. Rwanda's Mathias Ntawulikura was eighth in the 10,000 metres, and Dieudonné was astounded that a Rwandan had come eighth in the world. Ntawulikura's achievement inspired him, and awakened a desire to discover what achievements he himself might be capable of.

A few years later he was working in an office which overlooked a running track. Gazing at the track, he wondered how fast he could run, and soon discovered that the answer was very fast indeed. He became known as one of the best runners in Rwanda – a fact that was confirmed when he won a silver medal in the Junior African Games in 2000.

In 2004 he achieved the qualifying time for the Olympics and ran in the 10,000 metres in Athens. Though some athletes might have been disappointed at missing out on a medal, Dieudonné was philosophical, and took pride in the fact that he had qualified for the Games in the first place. "Because of my lack of experience, seventeenth was the best I could achieve in the Olympic final. I was not expecting to win a medal.

"I was not expecting to win a medal. Just getting to the Olympics was a big achievement in itself…"

Just getting to the Olympics was a big achievement in itself, as it is not easy to achieve the Olympic qualifying time."

His determination was rewarded the following year when he took gold and bronze in the Francophone Games. His victory took even the organisers by surprise – when it came to the presentation of his gold medal, they did not have the music for the Rwandan National Anthem so asked if he would mind if they played the All African anthem. He did mind, and so insisted on singing the anthem himself!

Dieudonné went on to compete in the 2008 Olympics, finishing nineteenth in the 10,000 metres, and in the 2010 Commonwealth Games Marathon (Rwanda was only accepted into the Commonwealth in 2009), where he did not finish because of injury.

"I knew that Jesus Christ was the answer."

Though successful in his sporting career, Dieudonné's life had been deeply affected by the loss of his family. He found himself questioning his beliefs, remembering his father praying on the day he died with the certainty that he was going to heaven. "In the Bible it says that there is only one way to heaven – Jesus Christ. If you are to get to heaven, it can only be through Jesus Christ. For me Jesus Christ is the way to heaven and the way to God.

After my family died I stopped praying and turned away from God. One day I realised that if I was ever going to see them again, I needed to start praying again. I knew that Jesus Christ was the answer and since then I have believed and prayed to him every day."

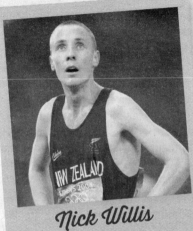

Nick Willis
NEW ZEALAND

For New Zealand born runner Nick Willis, 2012 was a year that combined career highs and lows. Nick came ninth in his event at the London Olympics – "heartbreaking," and also "a bit embarrassing," he admitted, especially as he had broken the New Zealand record earlier that year. It's a situation that will be familiar to other professional athletes, and one that Nick's Christian faith helps him cope with.

"Jesus gives me the security of his love and his promise in what he did for me – there is a much greater hope on the eternal side."

"Jesus gives me the security of his love and his promise in what he did for me – whether I was to come down with cancer today, my wife was to get hit by a car, whether I win or lose a race, whatever trials and tribulations happen in life, this is only a temporary existence. Because of what Jesus has done, there is a much greater hope on the eternal side."

When Nick won gold in the 1,500 metres in the 2006 Commonwealth Games, it was an unforgettable moment: "The 2006 Commonwealth Games was a great step forward. To get onto a podium and experience the sweet feeling of doing a victory lap and seeing so many people in your home country get so much pleasure out of your results, to realise you are not just running for yourself any more, was great. That gave me a huge hunger and desire to experience that again."

Sure enough, it was a feeling he would experience again, this time at the 2008 Olympics in Beijing. He finished third in the 1,500 metres, but when winner Rashid Ramzi was disqualified for a doping offence, Nick was promoted to the silver medal position. He said: "I was overjoyed with that as the pinnacle of my career. If I could never have run another step I would have been content. To have that experience was like nothing else. Of course, it was originally a bronze medal and then later I was elevated to silver after Rashid Ramzi's positive test. I wouldn't trade that experience for anything. I would love to get there again because that was just my little taste of heaven. To do something that you know is not possible in your own strength is a pretty incredible experience."

In the lead-up to the 2010 Commonwealth Games in Delhi, Nick wasn't on his best form thanks to knee surgery earlier in the year. However, he managed to walk away with bronze, coming third behind Kenyans Silas Kiplagat and James Magut. He has continued to build on his achievements, setting the Oceania 1500m record in 2012, and being chosen as the New Zealand Olympic flag bearer at London 2012.

Nick grew up in a Christian family but "tried to run away from what I thought were the rules and restrictions that being a Christian would place on my life. When you are a teenage boy, you are worried what people think." It wasn't until he left New Zealand to study and train in America that he changed his mind about Christianity, saying, "God put certain people into my life who helped me find the links in the chain and to show me by example that God isn't just some mystical figure up in the sky. They showed me that it was not just about going to church on Sunday but that Jesus was living inside these people". During this period he came to understand that his original view of being a Christian was wrong. He realized "that the things that I thought would be restrictions were actually freedoms and the true way to experience life."

Today, his Christian faith is an important and dynamic part of Nick's life, encapsulated by his approach to reading the Bible. "It is virtually impossible for me to read the Scriptures until I get right with God about what is going on in the day. It involves asking God 'What do you want to teach me today?' I can't just read the Bible just as a piece of information. It has life-giving qualities to it." Nick's attitude is proof that for him, and for many others, his faith in Jesus is more important than winning gold.

Christine Ohuruogu
ENGLAND

Christine Ohuruogu is undoubtedly one of Britain's greatest female athletes. She has been World Champion twice (2007 and 2013), Olympic champion in 2008 (and Olympic silver medallist in 2012) and Commonwealth Champion in 2006, in addition to winning five relay medals at major championships. When she broke the long-standing British record at the 2013 World Championships in Moscow, she said triumphantly, "The record is 29 years old – the same as me."

The Commonwealth Games have mixed memories for Christine. She won her first major medal there in 2006 in Melbourne. However, she also anchored the 4 by 400 metres relay team to first place, only for the team to be controversially disqualified over an alleged rule violation at a change-over. In 2010 injury prevented her from defending her Commonwealth title.

Christine's Christian faith plays a huge role in her life. After winning her gold medal in Moscow, the first thing she did was to thank God in a live BBC TV interview. She said afterwards, "I had been so aware of God's strength supporting me all week and I wanted to acknowledge that."

Christine says that for her, faith is something to hold on to through all the ups and downs of a professional athlete's life. "Sport is very fickle and when we rely on ourselves to do sport, that can really screw you up – especially when you are not doing what you are supposed to be doing. If you are not running what you should be running and you are not achieving what you should be achieving, it can really mess you up. And it is nice for me to know that there is a plan in place and whatever I do or achieve, there is always something bigger. It is good to be reminded of that. There are so many lessons that we can learn and that gives me a positive attitude and teaches me a lot about myself and how I am supposed to behave towards other people, competitors etc."

"Much as you want to beat your competitors, you have a more human way of looking at people."

She believes that having faith in God allows her to be more gracious in her sport. "Much as you want to beat your competitors, you have a more human way of looking at people, and respecting them. Jesus said we were to love our neighbours – even the ones who don't necessarily like us and we find hard to like."

Despite her packed schedule, Christine tries to make time for what is important to her away from her sporting career. "I have a church that I have always gone to. I like to go and sit quietly and set myself up for the

"I have a church that I have always gone to. I like to go and sit quietly and set myself up for the week."

week. It is always nice to remember what my position is, what my morals are, what my values are and to think about how I can implement them on a day-to-day basis – and not just on Sundays or when I go to church. It reminds me that we have to take our lives outside."

Christine's sporting career has many challenges, especially when it comes to performance under pressure. She admits, "I tend to worry a lot. I like it when Jesus says 'Come to me, all you who are weary and burdened, and I will give you rest.' (Matthew 11:28.) You can get inundated by everything that is happening. As a sportsperson you are being challenged every way possible – visually, physically – and you can get overwhelmed by everything that is going on, especially in a championship environment. But it is nice to have that safety net: if you are worried, come to me and it will be all right."

"Jesus says 'Come to me, all you who are weary and burdened, and I will give you rest.'"

If you have been inspired by reading
More Than Gold and would like to
discover more of the Bible go to:

www.pennygospel.org.uk

THE PENNY
Gospel ⓟ

**The Scottish Bible Society, 7 Hampton
Terrace, Edinburgh EH12 5XU,
t: 0131 337 9701
www.scottishbiblesociety.org**